THE MONSTER GARDEN

When Frankie persuades her brother to give her some of his stolen ''blob'' from the laboratory she doesn't believe it will grow into anything.

But overnight Frankie's blob begins to grow . . . and grow . . . and grow . . . until Frankie has her own baby monster!

How can Frankie hide her loving monster from her family? Can she trust any of her friends to keep her secret? And will Frankie be able to look after Monnie for ever?

ABOUT THE AUTHOR

Vivien Alcock was born in Worthing, Sussex and moved to Wiltshire when she was ten. She studied at Oxford School of Art and worked in London as a commercial artist for several years. She also did odd jobs as an ambulance driver, a secretary in a beauty salon and as a shop assistant in an antique shop.

Now she lives in Highgate in London with her husband, Leon Garfield, the well-known children's author, her daughter Jane and her dog and cat. She spends her time painting and writing.

She used to tell stories to her daughter and her friends and these grew into books for all children, including *The Haunting of Cassie Palmer* and *Ghostly Companions.*

THE
MONSTER GARDEN
Vivien Alcock

HEINEMANN
NEW WINDMILLS

Heinemann Educational Publishers
Halley Court, Jordan Hill, Oxford OX2 8EJ
a division of Reed Educational & Professional Publishing Ltd
MELBOURNE   AUCKLAND
FLORENCE   PRAGUE   MADRID   ATHENS
SINGAPORE   TOKYO   SAO PAULO
CHICAGO   PORTSMOUTH (NH)   MEXICO
IBADAN   GABORONE   JOHANNESBURG
KAMPALA   NAIROBI

ISBN 0 435 12349 1

97 98 99 2000 14 13 12 11 10 9 8

Cover illustration by Tracey Agate

Printed in England by Clays Ltd, St Ives plc

1

I shouldn't have done it. I didn't really mean to, but that's no excuse, of course. I should have known better with a name like mine. Frances Stein. Called Frankie for short.

The trouble was, I am a girl. My father is a high-up scientist and a low-down male chauvinist pig. You'd think with three sons he'd have been glad of a girl for a change, but he wasn't. He doesn't even know how to talk to females.

I suppose he must have spoken to my mother once, but she died when I was born, so I never heard him. He talks to Mrs Drake, our housekeeper, but she's old and flat, with grey hairs growing out of her chin, which she trims once a week with her nail scissors, so he may not have noticed she's a woman. Also the fact that her name is Drake and not Duck has probably confused him. Names are important.

Take mine – Frankie Stein. Frankenstein, they call me at school. You can't really blame me for making a monster. What did they expect me to do with a name like that?

I wanted to show my father that girls are as good as boys any day of the week. Better, in fact. I wanted him to notice me, not just pat me on the head and mumble and walk away. That's why I did it.

It was Thursday, the eighth of July. Our teachers were on a one-day strike so David and I were at home.

At least, I was at home, feeling cross and resentful because I had been left out again. My father had taken David to show him round the laboratories. I'd wanted to go too, but they said I was too young.

'You'd be bored,' David had said, with a horribly superior look on his spotted face. 'You wouldn't understand a thing and you'd start fidgeting and being a nuisance.'

What he meant was that I was only a girl and ought to be sitting at home and darning his socks. I'll see him dead before I touch his smelly socks! Looking so pleased with himself, the acne-d oaf. Thinking himself so clever –

No. That's not fair. David is my youngest older brother, and I know that he is secretly terrified that he won't do as well as Ben and Mike, who are both up at Cambridge now, flashing through their exams like express trains.

Poor David. He only came second in physics last term. Only second! The shame of it. The disgrace. He could hardly look my father in the eye.

I felt sorry for him, until he told me that women have smaller brains than men. What's size got to do with it? Elephants have enormous brains and I bet they still think the world is flat. (Actually it is rather flat at times, especially when you can't think of anything to do.)

I could not think what to do on that Thursday afternoon, the eighth of July. (The date is important. It was my monster's birthday.) My friends had rung up with various suggestions but I had refused them all.

I was in one of those sour, angry moods when you hug your misery to yourself and refuse to let anyone take it away. I wanted my father and David to come back and find me alone and neglected, preferably with tear-stains on my face, if I could manage it. Stupid of me. They wouldn't have noticed.

It was a hot, nasty day. The sky was dirty and the sun looked jaundiced. I was sitting sulking on my bed when I heard a noise in the passage outside. I got up and quietly opened the door.

David did not hear me. He was walking down the passage to his room in a peculiar, furtive sort of way. He was holding something in his pocket, and he moved his legs in a stiff glide, as if he was afraid whatever it was would spill.

It was obvious what he had done, the spotted snake. He had nicked something from Dad's laboratory. Interesting.

My father goes in for genetic engineering. If you don't know what that is, too bad, because I don't either. Nobody at home will explain it to me. They say I am too young to understand. And I only started doing science at school this year. We haven't got to genetic engineering yet. I asked Mr Tollington what it was, but I don't think he had a very clear idea either. It's true I did not hear every word he said, because Johnny Mason was drawing on my leg with a felt pen at the time and distracted me.

As far as I can gather, my father and the other scientists at the lab are playing about with living cells as if they were pieces of Lego. Separating them and adding them together in different patterns, growing babies in test tubes and tiny elephants in glass jars and trying to combine a sheep with a kangaroo. To be honest, I'm not sure if that's what Mr Tollington said. Unfortunately I missed most of it. But it's what the whole of 1A think. They call my father's laboratory a monster factory, and Debbie Scott says he tortures animals in it, which is not true. I asked David and he told me not to be silly. He said Dad was working for the good of mankind.

It still worried me. I suppose I should have asked my father but it is difficult to talk to him. He's not

3

unkind, he always smiles at me when he notices I'm there, but in a vague, puzzled way as if he knows he's seen me before but cannot quite remember who I am. I used to think that perhaps all scientists were like that, cold and remote. But they're not. Most of them are quite human.

I had to find out for myself. That's why I followed David along the passage, very quietly so that I wouldn't startle him and make him spill whatever he had in his pocket.

He has set up a mini-laboratory in his room, and keeps it locked so that I can't get in. But this time he was so excited he'd left the door open. I stood just outside and watched.

Very carefully, he took a test tube out of his pocket and put it in a rack on the table. Then he turned aside to get something out of a cupboard. I looked at the test tube. It was about a quarter full of some greyish, lumpy stuff like badly cooked porridge, only more transparent. It did not move.

David returned to the table and put down a petrie dish, (which is a sort of flat glass saucer). The bottom of it was coated with a red jelly. I knew what that was. Blood agar. You can grow germs on it if you want to. Personally, I do not.

Then he tipped the greyish goo from the test tube on to the petrie dish.

'What's that you've nicked?' I asked.

He swung round. His face at first went white, then bright red. Quite an interesting phenomenon.

'What the hell are you doing here, you little squirt?' he shouted, 'I told you never to come into my room.'

'If you use your eyes,' I said coldly, 'you may notice I'm not actually in your room. I'm just looking through your door. You'll never be a scientist unless you learn to observe data more carefully.'

He swore at me. He looked so angry I thought he was going to hit me, so I slipped past him and stood behind all his glass beakers and funnels and tubes. I knew he wouldn't risk breaking those. They are very expensive.

'Don't worry,' I said soothingly, 'I won't tell Dad.'

He swallowed whatever he'd been going to say, and his complexion faded from tomato sauce to strawberry ice-cream.

'On one condition,' I added.

'You stinking little toad,' he said wearily. 'I might have guessed. How much?'

'Half of that,' I said, pointing at the petrie dish.

He stared at me. 'Oh come on, Frankie,' he said, 'you don't even know what it is. I'll give you fifty pence.'

I shook my head.

'A pound.'

'No. I want some of that.'

'You little beast,' he said venomously. 'You're just doing it to spite me. You don't really want it. You wouldn't know what to do with it. As I said you don't even know what it is.'

'Living tissue,' I said hopefully. 'Cells and things.'

'And what good do you imagine it would do you if it were?' he asked scornfully. 'You haven't got an incubator. You haven't got a microscope. You haven't got anything, not even brains. It'd just be a waste. It'd be throwing the stuff away.'

'Either you give me some or I tell Dad.'

I was in a strong position. What David had done was pretty terrible, when you thought about it. I'd never have done it myself. I wouldn't have dared. Nicking something from a laboratory is a serious crime. Possibly a deadly one. Some of the stuff they keep in bottles is corrosive, which means that if you spill some on your hands, your flesh will burn and bubble right down to the bone. If David was found out, he'd be in real trouble.

I felt sorry for him now. Poor David. Trying to be as clever as Ben and Mike had driven him to dangerous lengths.

'You shouldn't have done it,' I said, not to be nasty but because I was worried.

'It was only waste. They were going to throw it out. They didn't want it,' he said defensively. 'I wouldn't have taken anything important.'

'But you didn't ask if you could have it, did you?'

'Yes! Yes, I did.'

'Liar,' I said. He was silent. I felt sorry for him and added more kindly, 'All right. Not half. Just a little bit, David, a very little bit.'

'Why on earth do you want it, Frankie? What for?'

'I want to grow a monster of my own,' I said.

I wasn't really serious. Just for once I didn't want to be left out of things. I don't know. Perhaps I hoped David and I might work together on some scientific project. If only I could prove that I wasn't an idiot just because I was young and female. If I could keep my bit of goo alive as long as he did his, he might be impressed. It was no more than that.

However, I admit I said the words – 'I want to grow a monster of my own.'

2

He was not exactly generous. The piece he gave me was no bigger than a single frog's egg. It looked rather like one, even down to a small dark nucleus in the centre.

'Are you sure it's not frogspawn?' I asked.

'Don't be silly.'

'Can I have a petrie dish and some of that blood agar stuff?'

'No. That wasn't part of our bargain. You just said some of this, and here it is,' he told me. 'Take it or leave it.' It was obvious which he hoped I would do.

'What can I carry it in?'

'Your hand.'

'No!' I put my hands behind my back.

'It won't bite, stupid,' he said, beginning to look comfortably superior again. He likes me to be silly. Poor David, with brothers like Mike and Ben, he needs someone to look down on. In the end he lent me a glass slide to carry it on. 'Only bring the slide back,' he said. 'They cost money.'

Once in my room again, I put the slide down on the table and looked round. Necessity, so they say, is the mother of invention. I hoped it would mother me.

My pot of African violets was standing in a saucer on the window sill. That would do. It was only a plain white saucer, slightly chipped, but we can't all be cradled in petrie dishes. My monster would have to rough it.

I washed and dried the saucer. Then I sterilized a needle in the flame of a match and pricked my thumb. I jabbed it harder than I meant to, and yelped. A scarlet bubble of blood appeared. I held my thumb over the saucer and squeezed.

I squeezed until my thumb ached, but the pool of blood, gleaming wetly in the sunlight, was disappointingly small. However, it would have to do. Carefully, I tipped the small grey lump into it. It quivered for a moment, like a jelly, and then lay still. It did not look alive. Oh, well!

I went to the Playhouse that evening with Hazel Brent and her parents. It was late when I got back. The sunlight had gone from the window sill. It was a hot night, dark and stuffy. I opened my window at the bottom without even noticing the saucer. My head was full of *My Fair Lady*.

'Da da dum dee dee,' I sang as I went to bed. 'Aow, wouldn't it be luverly.'

I'd completely forgotten about my monster.

It thundered in the night. I woke up and lay watching the lightning cracking the sky. How vivid it was. It made me blink. I am not in the least frightened of thunderstorms, coming as I do from a scientific family. But I had never seen lightning like this before. It came leaping towards my window as if it wanted to come in. So quick, so bright! It hurt my eyes.

So I shut them, and turning to face the wall, went back to sleep. I didn't remember that my window was still open at the bottom. I did not think of my monster at all. I didn't dream.

In the morning, I woke to the sound of water flushing through the cistern. (My room is next to the bathroom.) I heard the door open and shut and footsteps going down the passage. David. Then I remembered.

I sprang out of bed and ran over to the window. The saucer on the sill had cracked and was oddly blackened, as if it had been rubbed with soot. There was nothing in it. David was right. I was too young to be trusted to look after things.

Oh well, never mind, I thought.

It must have been very windy in the night. The window sill was still wet and one or two seed pods had blown on to it. The carpet felt damp under my feet. Then I noticed that all the petals had gone from the African violets, and the few leaves that remained were tattered as if –

I stepped back. *As if something had bitten pieces out of them!*

Then I saw it.

It was in the far corner of the window sill. Squatting there. Not moving. It had grown during the night. Now it was the size of one of those pale toadstools you find at the roots of trees in Burners Wood. Silvery grey in colour, humped in the middle and thinning towards a transparent, crinkled edge. While I slept, the dark spot in the centre must have grown and split. It now had two red eyes and they were looking at me.

Nonsense, I told myself. But I did not move.

It twitched.

Slowly, horribly, it began to squirm and slither over the sill towards one of the seed pods. Then it stopped. A growth came out of its side, like a short fat tentacle, and pounced. The tentacle drew back into the body. I saw the seed pod twist and wriggle as the grey, half-transparent flesh simmered around it like thick stew. Then it was gone.

I bit my lip hard. Interesting, I told myself. Fascinating. Instructive.

I hated it. I wished it were dead. I wanted to scrape it into a tin, tip it down the loo and pull the handle.

There was a tin on my dressing table but I didn't even pick it up. I knew I couldn't do it. I can't kill things. Not even things I dislike, like wasps and spiders and slugs. I'm too soft.

It is a flaw in my character, I suppose. David says that if you want to be a scientist, you cannot afford to be squeamish. You have to train yourself to think of the good of mankind, and forget that some small, shivering creature may enjoy the sunlight as much as you do.

I have tried to train myself. I once stood for ages in the garden, trying to be resolute and stamp on an ant. I raised my foot – but it was no good. The little ant looked so busy and happy, scurrying about in the green grass. I did not want my foot to blot out its sun, like a thunderbolt descending. After all, it hadn't done me any harm.

So I didn't flush the monster down the loo. Instead, I pricked my thumb again, in case it was thirsty.

'There you are,' I said, pushing it off the sill into the saucer with the corner of an envelope. 'Drinkies.'

It quivered and blushed. No. It wasn't blushing. It was the blood soaking up into the semi-transparent flesh. Ugh! It struck me then that perhaps it was not advisable to bring up a monster on my own blood. After all, I only had a limited supply. I didn't want it to develop a taste for it.

So before I went to school, I made a home for it in the empty aquarium that had once held my goldfish. I put in a small box with cotton wool for a bed, a bowl of milk and a large shallow dish filled with an assortment of food I filched from the larder when Mrs Drake was not looking. Brown bread, cold porridge, minced pork, cabbage leaves and some left-over apple sauce. Let it choose for itself. How was I to know what was good for it?

I left the house with David.

'How is your you-know-what getting on?' I asked.

'All right,' he said briefly. 'How's yours?'

'Flourishing,' I said.

He looked at me. I could see he didn't believe me. He probably thought I'd neglected it.

'What are you feeding yours on?' I asked.

'Blood agar,' he said, and snapped his mouth shut. He hates to be seen talking to me. I suppose he thinks it's demeaning, like being caught drinking milk instead of coffee. I could see his eyes searching the road for one of his friends.

'They eat a lot, don't they?' I asked, trying to hold his attention. 'Has yours grown much?'

'Oh, don't be so stupid,' he said impatiently. 'In one night? Of course it hasn't.' And he ran off down the pavement as if he couldn't bear my company a moment longer.

I was puzzled. It's true my monster was still comparatively small, but in one night it had more than doubled its size. Quadrupled it. Octopuddled, if there is such a word. And to do that on one spoonful of blood, an African violet and a few seed pods was no mean feat.

When I got back from school, I went straight up to my room. I had left the aquarium on my table. I took one look at it, slammed the door shut and ran down the passage as fast as I could.

'David! David! David!' I cried, hammering on his door.

3

No answer. The door was locked. That meant one of two things. Either David was out with the key in his pocket, or he'd locked himself in his room and was keeping quiet, hoping I'd go away and not bother him. Clever people can be very stupid. You see, when he's there, he leaves the key in the lock on the inside. All I have to do is look through the keyhole. If I see light, he's out. If my view is blocked, he's in. Simple, isn't it? Yet he never guesses how I know.

Today I could see a small patch of white wall and the edge of the table. I straightened up and kicked the door angrily. Trust David to be out when I needed him. I wanted to give him back his lump of dirty jelly. Now. This very minute. Hurry up, David. Don't dawdle back from school, discussing Einstein with your four-eyed friends. Don't stop at the library and strain your eyes over small print in huge books. This is your chance to get your missing piece of monster back.

I didn't want it any more. I didn't like it. I didn't like anything about it; its crimson eyes, its eating habits – and especially the way it kept growing and growing. It wasn't natural. Nothing could grow that quickly, and yet it had. It was now the size and shape of a small cushion, lolling against the glass of the aquarium, its grey flesh flattened out like a window-shopper's nose. Hurry back, David, and take it away.

'Frankie! Frankie!'

It was Mrs Drake, calling from the foot of the stairs.

I leaned over the banisters. 'Yes?'

'Tea's ready, dear.'

I went down. There was only me and Mrs Drake. On Fridays my father goes to his club and doesn't come back until long after I'm in bed. David was still out.

'Do you know when David will be back?' I asked Mrs Drake.

'No, dear. He didn't say. He never tells me anything.'

'He never tells me anything either,' I said, and we smiled at each other sympathetically. We get on quite well together, though I don't approve of the way she pampers my father and brothers, as if they belonged to a superior species, needing special care and devotion.

'I'm worried about that boy,' she said now. 'I think he's working too hard. He doesn't look at all well. He has dark shadows under his eyes.'

'That's just dirt,' I told her. 'Don't be fooled by the time he spends in the bathroom. He's washing out his beakers and test tubes, not his face. You could grow cress on the back of his neck.'

She shook her head at me. 'Still, you break up from school on Wednesday, don't you?' she said. 'He'll be able to sleep in, poor boy.'

We have high tea. Today it was ham salad, followed by a green jelly, with bits of banana suspended in it. It lolled and quivered on my plate.

I swallowed hard, and pushed the plate away.

'What's the matter, dear? Don't you want it? It's usually your favourite.'

'I don't feel hungry. It's too hot.'

It never occurred to me to confide in her. I knew she would tell my father. She's a terrible tell-tale, but I forgive her, because I know she's fond of me and only does it for my own good. It's just a pity that her idea of what is good for me is so completely different from my own. You wouldn't think anybody could be so wrong.

After tea we watched television until it was time for our nightly argument.

'Come on, Frankie. You promised to go to bed when this finished.'

'I want to see what's on next.'

'No, dear. A promise is a promise.'

'It's not fair. David isn't even home yet.'

'He's over four years older than you,' she pointed out. 'Besides, he's a boy.'

'What difference does that make?' I asked furiously.

'Girls need their beauty sleep,' she said smugly, sitting there, so old and ugly, with whiskers growing out of her chin and her legs as thin as knitting needles. I nearly asked her if, when she was a girl, her mother had kept her awake all night, but I didn't have the heart to. I felt so sorry for her. She's not a bad old stick.

So I kissed her goodnight, and went upstairs. I looked at my closed door. Come on, Frankie, I told myself, you're not afraid of a lump of jelly, are you?

A scientist has to be honest. The answer to that was 'Yes'.

I put my ear to the door and listened. Silence. Well, what did I expect it to do? Sing?

I went in.

The monster had not moved. It was still lolling against the glass of the aquarium.

I crept closer. It was lying on its back. Its eyes, fixed and staring, were no longer red but milky pink. I bent nearer and saw that they were covered with a silvery transparent skin, like clingfilm. It looked dead. Very dead. I tapped on the glass, softly at first and then harder, but it did not stir. There was no sign that it was breathing.

14

Dead as a doornail.

Oh well. Never mind, I thought. Perhaps it was all for the best. A merciful relief, as Mrs Drake had said, when her old aunt died.

Tomorrow I would bury it in the garden, next to the graves of my goldfish, and recite something suitably sad. 'Monster, rest in peace. May the sun warm the earth you sleep in, and the birds sing you lullabies.' I would give it a good send-off, poor creature.

I slept well that night, though I had an odd dream. I dreamed that the roof of our house exploded into the sky, and the bricks came crashing down with a roar like thunder. Then suddenly the dream changed, as dreams do. The house was gone and before me there was only a wide field of pink grass, on which a bed stood by itself under the white sky. I walked slowly towards the bed and looked down. Someone was sleeping in it, her hair spread out like brown water over the pillow. I stared at her. So that was how I should look. I put out my hand . . .

Something touched my cheek and I woke up.

The monster was sitting on my pillow, looking at me, its face only a few inches from my own.

4

I shot out of bed so fast that I must have broken the sound barrier. When I opened my mouth and screamed, no sound came out.

I stood with my back to the window. I was trapped. It was between me and the door.

The monster sat on the pillow and stared at me with its red eyes. It had changed again. It was now – most horribly, grotesquely – half human in shape. It had a domed head, but no hair, no nose, no ears. It had two eyes and a thin slit of a mouth, as if someone had drawn a line in soft clay with a knife; a thick body, short stumpy arms and legs. But no hands or feet. Its grey flesh had a greenish tinge. It looked absurdly like a very large jelly-baby.

'Go away!' I shouted. My voice cracked and crackled in my throat like cornflakes. I stamped on the floor and shook my fist at it threateningly.

It scuttled off the bed, across the carpet and hid under the table. The lid had come off the aquarium and was lying on the floor, upside down. It crouched behind it, but it was too big. Its bottom stuck up in the air and trembled.

I took a step towards the door but my knees gave way and I collapsed on to the bed. I sat there, with my legs tucked under me, trying to recover my strength. I was afraid I was going to faint.

The monster peeped at me from behind the lid and

ducked down again. It did this three times, and then, emboldened perhaps because I did not move, it came out from behind its barrier, crawling on all fours like a baby.

'Go away!' I shouted, waving my arms.

It scuttled back immediately, falling into the lid in its hurry, so that its stupid short legs stuck up into the air.

I laughed. I expect I was hysterical. Or mad. I can't think of any other reason why I didn't scream and run from the room like any sane person would have done. I just sat on my bed and watched it.

It was playing now. It sat in the upside-down lid as if in a boat, and rocked backwards and forwards until the lid tilted too far and tumbled it on to the floor. It seemed to enjoy this for it did it several times.

Then it looked at me. Its eyes were very round and a clear light crimson. Quite a pretty colour, really. It began twisting its slit of a mouth in a most ridiculous manner. Now it would bend the corners down until it looked like a croquet hoop; now up into a capital U. Once it even managed to twist it into a figure eight. I couldn't help laughing at it. It didn't seem to know what a mouth was for. It never opened it, not once. Perhaps it wasn't a proper mouth at all.

Now it stood up and started stretching its legs. I don't mean the way we stretch them, but like elastic. Its fat, short stumps grew longer and thinner until they couldn't bear the weight of its body and it fell down. Its legs shrank back to their previous size and it sat up and looked at them and then at me, as if puzzled.

I laughed again.

Someone knocked at my door.

'Don't come in!' I shouted, and the monster scuttled back under the table again and hid. It seemed surprisingly timid for a monster.

'Breakfast!' David called through the door. 'Didn't you hear Mrs Drake shouting? She wants you down pronto. Your scrambled egg's getting cold.'

'I won't be a minute.'

I waited till I heard him going downstairs. Then I looked at my monster, wondering what to do. I could have let David in. I could have asked him to take it back. I don't quite know why I didn't. I needed time to think.

The food and milk had all gone. So were all the leaves from my rubber plant, which probably accounted for the monster's greenish hue. I filled the dish with water and put it down on the floor. I waited. The monster recovered from its fright and peeped out at me.

'Drink,' I said loudly, pointing to the dish. 'I'll bring you something to eat later, if you're good.'

It just stared. I don't suppose it heard a word I said. After all, it had no ears.

I went out of my room, locked the door behind me and put the key in my pocket. Then I went downstairs.

I was very quiet at breakfast. Nobody noticed. Mrs Drake was busy rushing backwards and forwards from the kitchen, and as usual my father and David didn't talk to me.

My father was reading the paper and did not even look up when I came into the room. This is usual. Ben, who is my oldest and nicest brother, says I mustn't mind. He says Dad has such enormous powers of concentration that when he's thinking of one thing, he completely shuts everything else out of his mind. Such as me. He wasn't being rude or unkind, Ben said. He just did not know I was there.

David knew. He looked up when I came in, but looked away without a word. He had a large book on biochemistry which he was pretending to read, in order to impress our father. I'm sure Dad didn't notice that either.

Usually I say 'Good morning' very loudly to make them jump, but not today. I was glad to sit silently at the table, trying to decide what to do. I could not cope with an expanding monster all on my own. I would have to tell someone, but who? Not my father. I had promised David I would not tell him, and I never break my promises if I can help it. David? Possibly. I looked at him. He was pale. His eyes were heavy and slightly bloodshot. Mrs Drake was right. He didn't look well. He kept frowning over his book, though I didn't think he was actually reading it. His eyes did not move backwards and forwards but were fixed in a gloomy stare. Perhaps he was worried, too. He'd kept the lion's share of the monster stuff, after all. I wondered uneasily what size his had grown to now.

After breakfast, I followed him up to his room.

'David –'

'What is it, Frankie? Can't it wait? I have to go out and I'm late already.'

'You know that stuff you gave me?'

'What about it?' he asked irritably, unlocking and opening his door. I tried to peer past him, but he was in the way.

'What's yours like now?' I asked. 'Has it grown arms and legs? Has it got red eyes?'

'Oh, for God's sake, Frankie, try not to be so silly. I'm in a hurry –'

'I'm not being silly. Please, David. I can't help being worried,' I cried, catching hold of his arm. 'Why won't you tell me what it's like?'

'It's dead,' he said shortly, pulling his arms away.

'Dead?'

'I expect it was dead when I got it. That's probably why he put it out to be got rid of. Something must've gone wrong –'

'It might be asleep,' I suggested, remembering how I thought mine was dead last night.

'I told you. It's dead,' he said impatiently. 'Come in and see if you don't believe me. Only don't break anything.'

On his table, beside his microscope, was a razor blade and a mess of crumbled fragments of greyish jelly.

'What have you done to it?' I cried, staring.

'I was trying to cut sections for my slides, but it's impossible without the proper equipment. You can't cut it thin enough by hand,' he said gloomily. 'I should have tried setting it in wax first. Or freezing it. It's too late now. I haven't any left.'

I looked at the tiny fragments in horror, feeling sick.

'Are you sure that it was really dead before you cut it up?'

'Of course I'm sure. I'm not stupid, Frankie –' He broke off and looked at me hopefully, 'What about the bit I gave you? Have you still got it?'

'It's dead, too,' I said ʳⁱckly. 'I flushed it down the loo. It's gone.'

It was no good, you see. I could not hand over my timid, ridiculous baby monster to David. I did not trust him to look after it properly.

I left his room, and stood on the landing, looking down over the banisters. It was very quiet. The hall was dim and shadowy, like the inside of my head. I could not think what to do. Ben and Mike were out of reach, somewhere in France. I couldn't wait for them to come back. My monster was growing too quickly.

I'd just have to find someone else to help me. One of my friends.

20

5

My friends. I thought about them.

Hazel Brent is my best friend. She has black curly hair, bright black eyes, and very white teeth in a nut-brown face. She is always laughing. To be honest, she is rather frivolous. That's why I like her so much. She's fun to be with. I get tired of solemn, silent people. I have too much of that at home.

If I told Hazel about my problem, she would shriek and giggle and tell the world. I could just see her dancing around the playground on Monday, chanting, 'Frankie's got a monster! Frankie's got a monster!'

No. I sighed.

I went through my other friends in my mind. No. No. No. Nothing but noes. I had chosen my friends too carelessly, just because I liked them, not for use. I couldn't trust one of them to keep a secret. They were all lively, light-hearted chatter-boxes. Not one earnest, tight-lipped, secretive so-and-so among the lot.

Oh, well.

In the end, I decided to tell Julia Hobson. She was in my class at school, though I did not know her very well. I'd often thought she wanted us to be friends, but I'd considered her a bit too quiet and serious for my taste. However, she was calm and clever, good with animals and babies, and that was what I needed now. Also she had a brother, John, who was in the form above us and was said to be good at languages.

I went round to see them without going back to my room. They were still having breakfast. Their mother let me in and sat me down at the table, and after offering me coffee, which I refused, gave me some milk.

Julia smiled as if she was pleased to see me, but was obviously wondering why I had come. We'd never visited each other's houses before. She had asked me to tea once or twice, but I had always made some excuse.

'I'm sorry to barge in so early,' I began, a little nervously, for I hadn't expected to have them all there listening to me.

'Not at all, my dear,' Mrs Hobson said politely. 'You're very welcome, I'm sure.'

'I – I wanted to ask Julia something.'

Julia smiled and waited. They all waited. Even Mr Hobson looked up from his paper.

What was I to say? They were such a pleasant, kind, ordinary family. It was Saturday morning and the sun was shining. Cars were passing in the street outside, and I could hear the voices of children playing. A ginger cat lay on the window-sill, its eyes half-shut in contentment.

How could I talk of monsters?

'I want – I need some help,' I said. 'It's just . . . I've been doing an experiment in my room, and it's gone a bit wrong.'

'You haven't blown the roof off your house, have you?' Mr Hobson asked, perhaps hopefully. (He is a builder.)

'No,' I said, smiling politely. I suppose he was joking. 'It's just turned out – well, a bit odd. I thought Julia could advise me. She always comes top in class.'

'I'm not very good at science,' Julia said modestly. 'Not like your brothers. Can't David help you? Or your dad?'

'They're out,' I said shortly.

'Of course, I'd like to help you, Frankie, if I can,' Julia said quickly, afraid that she had offended me. 'It was just that we haven't been doing science long. That's all. I'd like to help.'

'What's the problem?' Mr Hobson asked.

'It's difficult to describe,' I said evasively. 'I wondered if Julia could come back with me and I could show it to her. We're only just round the corner in Hailsham Road.'

'I know,' Mr Hobson said. He was frowning. Perhaps he was wondering why I had never asked Julia round before, when we lived so close. 'What sort of experiment is this you're talking about? You're not playing around with chemicals, I hope. You could hurt yourselves that way.'

'It's nothing like that,' I assured him. 'It's only . . . something in my aquarium. A sort of pet. I think I may have been feeding it the wrong things – and Julia's so good with pets. I mean, you've got a dog and cats and guinea pigs and goldfish . . .'

'Oh, a sick fish,' he said. 'That's all right then.'

They all smiled at me. Julia said she had some fish food and an anti-fungus medicine in her room and went to fetch it. Mrs Hobson cleared the breakfast things on to a tray and bore them off to the kitchen, refusing my offer of help. Mr Hobson went out to mow the lawn. I was left alone with John. Good.

He is a tall, freckle-faced boy, with thick brown hair which he wears in a long fringe, hiding his eyebrows. I'd always rather liked the look of him, though I don't suppose he'd even noticed me. He looked utterly astonished when I asked him if he would come too.

'*Me?*' he asked.

'Yes.' I flushed a little, hoping he would not imagine I was sweet on him. 'You see, you're good at

23

languages, and it might come in useful . . .' I tailed off unhappily. It was obvious from his expression that he was wondering if I were mad.

'You mean you want me to talk to a fish? In French? Or would it prefer German, do you think?'

'It's not a fish. Not exactly.'

Julia came back then, carrying a plastic bag.

'You can put away your fish food and medicine,' her brother told her. 'Apparently it isn't a fish, after all.'

'What is it, then?' she asked, puzzled.

I hesitated.

'A lizard? A snake?'

'Not exactly. I wish you'd come and see it.'

They exchanged glances, the sort of glances it's only too easy to read. They might just as well have said aloud, 'What's she up to? Is she mad?'

'If I tell you, will you promise not to tell anyone else?' I asked. 'Will you promise faithfully? Will you swear not to?'

'Cross my heart and spit and hope to die,' Julia said, smiling. We both looked at John.

He shrugged. 'All right. Cross my heart and all the rest of it.'

He sounded as if he were humouring an idiot. I must have looked doubtful, because Julia said quickly, 'You can trust him.'

So I told them. I told them about David's stealing the test tube of goo from the laboratory. I told them how I'd forced him to give me a bit. I told them how his had died, but mine had grown. Had changed . . .

'What's it like now?' they asked curiously, not certain whether to believe me.

'Come and see,' I said. 'Please.'

So the three of us set off together in the morning sunlight. The world looked so warm and cosy and safe. Monsters did not belong in this bright suburb, with its neat gardens rich with roses and lavender and cats. You could not even see the laboratories from here, though I always felt they cast a shadow over the whole town.

I began to wonder if the whole thing was a dream. Or like the sort of toothache that drives you to the dentist, and then vanishes the moment you're in the waiting room and it's too late to change your mind. I began to worry that when I opened my bedroom door, I would have nothing to show them but an empty room.

6

'I can't see anything,' John said, 'There's nothing in here.'

They were both looking into the aquarium, puzzled and suspicious, as if they thought I was playing a silly joke.

'It's hiding under the table,' I told them.

I had seen it the minute we entered the room, but then I knew where to look. The monster was curled up tight in the corner. It looked shapeless and did not move. I thought it was terrified. It must have heard our footsteps clattering up the stairs, or felt the vibrations, perhaps. I did not know how it worked.

John and Julia squatted down and peered into the dark shadow under the table.

'Where . . .? Move over, John, I can't see . . . What's that? Is that it?' Julia asked doubtfully.

'Very funny,' John said, sounding unamused. 'How many packets of jelly did you use for this work of art, Frankie? It is jelly, isn't it?'

He leaned forward and poked it with his finger.

The monster shot out from under the table, across the pink carpet and disappeared under my bed.

They cried out in horror. Julia put her hand over her mouth and backed away until she was up against the window-sill and had no further to go. John held his ground, but his face had gone so white that his freckles stood out like pepper on boiled cod. There was a look of sick revulsion on both their faces.

I was furious!

A wave of some new, strange feeling made my cheeks burn. I wanted to cry. I wanted to shout at them. I couldn't understand it – until I remembered poor Mrs Peck.

Mrs Peck has the ugliest baby you've ever seen. An oozing, snuffling swamp of a baby, covered with spots and cold sores, snot and dribble. When people look into its pram, they tie their tongues into knots trying to be polite. 'He'll grow out of it,' Mrs Drake had told her kindly. 'I'd a nephew who was ugly as a baby, but he's now the sweetest –'

'What do you mean – ugly?' Mrs Peck had shrieked.

Poor Mrs Peck, I had laughed at her then. Now I knew how she felt. How dared they look at my poor monster like that? It wasn't ugly. It was – unusual, that was all.

I had never had a proper pet before, only goldfish, which somehow aren't the same. I never knew they could make you feel like this.

'Now you've gone and frightened it,' I said angrily, kneeling down and peering under the bed.

'Careful, Frankie!' John cried. 'It could sting – for God's sake, we'd better get out of here quick.'

'You can go if you like,' I said coldly. 'Only remember you promised not to tell.'

'We can't leave you here with – with *that*,' he said. I suppose it was noble of him, but I'm afraid I wasn't very grateful.

Looking at him, I saw that he was examining his finger anxiously, rubbing it on his jeans and then peering at it again.

'Would you like some sandpaper?' I asked. 'Or I could cut your finger off, if it'll make you feel happier.'

He flushed. 'Have you actually touched that – that creature, Frankie?'

'No,' I admitted.

'Then how do you know it isn't poisonous?'

I didn't, of course.

'Sorry,' I muttered, ashamed. 'Would you like a wash? The bathroom's next door. On the left. There's some Dettol on the shelf.'

'No, it's all right,' he said stiffly. I had hurt his pride. He'd rather die now than wash his finger.

I wished I'd never told them. I looked at Julia. She was still pale and had one hand pressed against her mouth. I had thought she was calm and sensible and clever. Now she looked sick and silly. I suppose I ought to have warned them what to expect. After all, I'd been frightened of it at first.

'It won't hurt you,' I said. 'It's only a baby and very timid.'

They looked at me as if I were mad. Then Julia gave a muffled shriek. Her eys widened. I looked around. The monster was creeping out from under the bed, very slowly. It stared at them. Then it stood up, wobbling a little on its feetless legs, and tottered towards me, holding out its arms.

I jerked away from it. I couldn't help it.

It stopped immediately. It looked at me. There were no tears in its crimson eyes, no expression I could recognise on its alien face. It made no sound. Yet somehow I felt grief and bewilderment flooding out of it like an invisible current. It might have been any or every lost and frightened child.

I forced myself to hold out my hands to it, and saw with shame that they trembled.

It hesitated for a moment, and then staggered into my arms. I held it gently and stroked its poor, bald head. To my relief, its flesh was not slimy, but cool and firmer than I had expected. I looked across at John, smiling with bravado, although already I was imagining that the palm of my hand itched and burned.

'You see?' I said. 'It's quite all right.'

'You're mad, Frankie,' he said, but I heard an unwilling admiration in his voice and was pleased.

'I don't think you should touch it, Frankie,' Julia said. 'Honestly I don't. I think you're being very silly. You don't know what they do in the laboratories. None of us knows. They could be making secret weapons –'

I laughed and even John smiled at this. Julia flushed.

'How do you know they're not? They must be up to something nasty or they wouldn't be so secret about it. All those wire fences and guard dogs, it's obvious they've got something to hide. Haven't you ever heard of germ warfare?'

'It's a trifle on the large side for a germ, Julia,' John said. I was glad to see he had recovered his nerve. The monster was now sitting on the floor beside me, looking at my hands and then at its own handless stumps, as if realising something was missing. 'I don't know what it is,' John went on. 'But I can't help thinking it's one of their mistakes.'

'You'll have to tell your father,' Julia said. 'You'll have to give it back.'

'No!'

'I think you'll have to, Frankie,' John said. 'You can't keep a thing like this hidden. Not the way you say it's been growing. And Julia's right. It could be dangerous.'

'I promised David I wouldn't tell Dad. And I always keep my promises,' I added pointedly, to remind them of theirs.

They were silent, thinking about it. Their faces were a better colour now. The sight of the monster, sitting quietly on the floor, looking at my hands and then at theirs with the mild interest of a baby, had reassured them.

'You wouldn't have to tell your father,' John said at last. 'You could take it to the laboratory yourself and pretend you found it wandering about outside.'

'I don't trust them,' I said.

He bit his lip. They knew what I meant. They had heard the rumours too. David had said it was nonsense and quite untrue. But how was I to know? My father had never taken me round the laboratories. Why not?

Julia gasped suddenly, and stared. I turned round.

The monster had grown two round pudgy hands on the end of its arms and was now attempting fingers. It could not count. Not five, not fifty, but hundreds of thin silvery threads appeared as we watched, fringing each hand till they looked like sea anemonies. It held them out to show us and twisted its mouth into a figure eight.

'It's certainly no mathematician, is it?' John said with a shaky laugh.

The monster looked at him. (It must be able to hear, I thought.) It looked at him and changed its mouth into a U.

'Look! It's smiling,' John said, staring in astonishment. 'Did you see that, Frankie? It smiled at me.'

I knew it was probably only a coincidence, but I did not tell him this. 'It's got a very nice nature,' I said.

It's strange what a smile, even an accidental one, can do. From that moment, John never looked at my monster with sick horror again. He still thought I should give it up, but he was half won over. I know he was. I wouldn't have any trouble with him.

I wished I could be certain about Julia.

7

We were sitting round the kitchen table, having a conference. I'd offered them milk and biscuits, but they had both refused. I think they were still feeling churned up inside. The monster was asleep, safely locked in my room. No. I mustn't keep calling it a monster. Names are important. I did not want it to grow up with the wrong idea. I'd call it Monnie. That sounded like a name. Perhaps if I'd called it Monnie from the start, Julia would not be so against it now.

'It's no good, Frankie,' she said. 'You can't keep it. You'll have to tell your father.'

'No.'

'David, then.'

'No.'

'One of the teachers. Mr Tollington –'

'No.'

'Why not, Frankie?' John asked, 'It's not a bad idea. He's OK.'

'He'd make me give it back to the laboratory.'

'I'm sorry, Frankie, but I think that's where it belongs,' Julia said. I was beginning to dislike her. 'It's not a proper animal. It's just something they made up in the lab – like nylon or polyester. I mean, it hasn't got a soul.'

'I think it has,' I said.

She looked at me and sighed ostentatiously. 'Really, Frankie –'

'I *do*. The first night I had it, there was that weird thunderstorm, remember? Did you hear it? Did you see the lightning, how bright it was? My window was open at the bottom, and I'd left the – the jelly in a saucer on the sill. I'd forgotten all about it. It was tiny then, no bigger than a frog's egg. I think God was sorry for it and touched it with his finger. Whoever made the monster, I think it's God's creature now,' I said, hoping to shift some of the blame.

They stared at me doubtfully.

'Come off it, Frankie,' John said, looking embarrassed.

Julia was silent. I don't know if she believed me. I wasn't certain whether I believed it myself.

'I can't let them destroy it. I can't. I've got to look after it. I know it's difficult, especially if it keeps growing so fast. But I think it's slowed down. It's difficult to tell because it changed its shape. But I don't think it's much bigger. If only I can hide it somewhere till Ben comes back from France. That's only eight days. I know he'll help me. He's brilliant. Everyone says so. He'll be able to think of a way to save it.'

'Oh,' Julia said, her face clearing. 'I didn't realise you were going to tell anyone. Ben's one of your brothers, isn't he?'

I nodded. 'The oldest. And the nicest.'

'That makes all the difference,' she said. 'If it's only just over a week. What do you think, John?'

'Don't see why not,' he agreed cheerfully. 'Harmless little beast. Friendly. Pity it hasn't got fur, though.'

'Rabbits don't have fur when they're born.'

He laughed and shook his head. 'Sorry to disappoint you, Frankie, but whatever it is, it's certainly no rabbit. I wonder what they were trying to make. An edible jellyfish, perhaps.'

'No,' I said indignantly.

'Perhaps you're right. I wouldn't fancy eating it, would you?'

'I wish you'd shut up,' Julia said, looking queasy again. 'It's not funny. We've got to decide what to do. Where were you thinking of keeping it, Frankie?'

That was the trouble. I didn't know. I could lock it in Ben's room for tonight and tomorrow, but on Monday I had to go to school. We didn't break up till Wednesday. Three days ... I couldn't leave it alone in the house. It might thump about above Mrs Drake's head and she'd think it was burglars and call the police. I needed a safe hiding place.

'Haven't you got a garden shed?' John asked.

'Yes, but it's right by the kitchen.' I pointed. 'Mrs Drake keeps potatoes and tins and things in it. It wouldn't be safe. I suppose you haven't got anywhere?'

'No,' they said, very firmly.

'What about a rabbit hutch at the bottom of your garden?' John suggested. 'Have you got an old one?'

'No. Perhaps I could buy one. Are they very expensive?'

'Bound to be. Things always are. Anyway, it's no good,' he said. He was standing up and looking through the window. Our square lawn was edged by narrow flower beds, in which red geraniums stood in line like soldiers guarding the stone walls. 'It's too tidy. They'd see it at once and want to know what you'd got in there.'

'Our garden goes on beyond that hedge at the bottom,' I told him. 'There're some steps in that corner leading down to a bit of rough ground. It's where we have our compost heap and bonfires. It'd be quite secret. Mrs Drake never goes beyond the terrace, her feet hurt. And Dad and David aren't interested in gardens. No one ever goes there, except me – and Alf, of course.'

'Alf? Who's Alf?' they asked.

'He's a jobbing gardener. We have him one afternoon a week. This afternoon, in fact. I wonder . . .' I said. 'I wonder if I should tell him?'

Julia advised me against it, and gave me a lot of reasons why not. I didn't listen to them. I was thinking about Alf, and her voice was no more than a fly buzzing in the background. An irritating fly. If only I'd thought of Alf sooner, I could have done without her altogether.

I liked Alf. He is a slow, cheerful man, who always wears a straw hat, summer or winter. He has one of those curved mouths like a child's drawing of a smile, and fingernails full of earth. David says he's simple, but he's not. He knows all about plants and animals, and they seem to know him too, and brighten up when he's there.

I told David so, but he just shrugged. He's so conceited he thinks the only knowledge worth having is the sort he's got himself.

Alf lives with his old, bedridden mother in a house near the railway line, and keeps rabbits. Hazel and I went to tea with them once, and Alf took us down to see his rabbits. He's very proud of them. They live in wooden hutches he has made himself, and have large wire runs so that they can enjoy the dappled sunlight. I was surprised when I saw his garden, it was so untidy. He keeps ours like a parade ground, very neat and everything in rows. Perhaps he thinks we like it that way. His own is wild and overgrown, full of trees and bushes and dandelions, all growing where they please.

I was sure Alf would make me a hutch if I asked him to. I'd have to get the wood and wire netting . . .

I looked at John and Julia hopefully. Their father was a builder. His yard was piled up with planks of wood.

Julia was shocked when I asked.

'Wood's very expensive, Frankie,' she said. 'You can't expect Dad to give it away. Why should he? It's not as if we're best friends, is it?'

'No,' I agreed, and was surprised to find this answer displeased her. Perhaps I had said it too loudly, but what did she expect? She knew that Hazel was my best friend.

'Oh, come on, Julia,' John said. 'Dad's got lots of scrap wood from demolition jobs. You know he'd let us have some. We can bring it over this afternoon. But how will you explain what we want it for, Frankie?'

'There's a door in the garden wall back there. On to Thurlow Street. They won't know if we come in that way. You can't see behind the hedge, not even from the upstairs windows, because of the trees.'

'They'll hear us hammering.'

'I'll say we're making something for school. They won't be interested.'

'What will you tell your gardener? The same thing?'

'I don't know,' I said slowly.

'You can't tell him the truth, Frankie,' Julia said. 'You can't even let him see that creature. He'd guess at once where it came from, anyone would, and he'd be bound to tell your father. He'd be afraid of getting into trouble if they ever found out. He wouldn't dare keep it quiet.'

'Yes, he would. You don't know him. He's not like them. Besides, they wouldn't blame him if they found out. They'd blame me. I'm sure I can trust him. He's my friend. He'll be on my side.'

Julia was staring at me. 'Alf? Isn't he that silly old man who wears a straw hat all the time? Even when it rains? Frankie, you can't mean to tell *him*! He looks half-witted.'

Now I knew I hated her. I opened my mouth to tell her so – John nudged me under the table, and I shut it

35

again. He was right. I had let Julia into my secret, and however much I regretted it now, I could not afford to quarrel with her. Not if I wanted to keep Monnie safe.

8

'Four small meals a day,' Julia told me firmly before they left. '*Small* ones, Frankie. Not more than about three or four ounces at a time. Plenty of fresh water and milk. And a litter tray –'

'I don't think it does anything.'

'Don't be silly. Of course it must. You'd better wash your carpet with disinfectant. Small animals are very messy. The sooner we get that hutch made the better. Call for us at three and don't be late.'

'I'll have the wood ready,' John promised. 'You can help us carry it round.' He smiled at me. 'Poor Frankie. You look tired already.'

'It's no good having a pet unless you're prepared to look after it properly,' Julia said.

She had had a lot of experience. Their cat was always having kittens. I suppose I should have been grateful for her advice.

I don't think Monnie was. It looked at the small saucer of grated cheese and carrot and chopped spinach, and glanced at me as if to say, 'Is that all?' Then it put its left leg into the saucer.

'No, Monnie, you're supposed to eat it –' I began. Then I broke off and turned away, feeling slightly sick. I don't know why absorbing your food through your leg should be worse than putting it in your mouth and chomping it with your teeth, but somehow I could not bear to watch. I began washing my carpet with disinfectant, sighing heavily, wishing I had never started all this.

When I had finished, the monster had gone to sleep in the lid of the aquarium, its crimson eyes silvered over by the transparent film. Its arms were crossed on its chest. I noticed it now had two fingers on one hand and about twenty or so on the other. I could not help smiling. Then I looked curiously at its legs. At the end of each one, where the feet should have been, there was a circular depression, larger than a tenpenny piece, closed at the bottom by two plump, puckered folds of flesh.

Like lips, I thought, and shrank away, a little frightened again. It was so strange, so very alien. What did I know about it? Perhaps Julia was right, and it was dangerous . . .

Then it stirred lazily in its sleep, and its mouth curved up as if it were smiling. It looked very peaceful. Very young.

I tiptoed from my room, locked the door and went down to the garden.

Mrs Drake was sitting in a deckchair on the terrace. Her knitting had fallen on to her lap and she was dozing. On the other side of the lawn, Alf was bending over a flower bed. My father and David were out. Now was the time.

I crossed the grass and squatted down beside Alf, who smiled at me from under the brim of his straw hat.

'Lot of weeds come up, Frankie,' he said. 'The storm we had a couple of nights ago, that's what done it. Lot of weeds.'

I watched him pulling them up. 'Do you ever feel sorry for them?' I asked.

'Don't get what you mean, Frankie,' he said after a pause. 'Sorry for who?'

'The weeds.'

He thought about it for a moment. 'They're weeds,' he said at last. 'Got to come up. This is a flower bed. Can't have weeds growing in a flower bed, can we?'

'I suppose not.'

'I get what you mean now,' he said. 'They're living things too. Still, this isn't the place for them. This is a flower bed.'

I was silent, thinking about my monster and wondering where was the right place for it to grow.

'Can you keep a secret, Alf?' I asked.

'Ah, secrets, is it?' he said, putting one finger against the side of his nose. 'I like secrets.'

'But can you keep them?'

'Yes. You can tell me, Frankie. I'm good at secrets. I won't tell no one, I promise. Not even my old mum. What's it all about, then?'

I hesitated, and then said, 'Can you make me a rabbit hutch in secret – behind the hedge – so that nobody knows anything about it?'

'A secret rabbit hutch, eh?' he said, and his smile widened to show his crooked teeth. 'What you going to have in it, then? Secret rabbits, Frankie? Secret rabbits?' He laughed loudly at this idea, and I glanced anxiously towards the terrace. Mrs Drake was still asleep.

'Mustn't wake her, must we?' Alf said, lowering his voice to a whisper. 'So you want a secret rabbit, Frankie. Won't your dad let you have one, then?'

'It's not a rabbit exactly,' I told him. 'It's a very rare animal. There's not another like it in the country. It's very unusual. I – er – want to give it to David for his birthday.'

'I get you. It's to be a surprise, eh?'

'Yes,' I said, biting my lip to hide a smile. 'That's it. A surprise.'

'When's his birthday, then?'

'Oh – not yet.'

Alf sat back on his heels, looking at me. He'd pushed his straw hat back on his head, and his blue eyes were uncomfortably sharp. 'I had a bit of his birthday cake – when was it now? After my Whitsun break, that's it. I come back from Bournemouth on the Tuesday and it was the next Saturday – May, that's when it was.'

'Yes,' I admitted.

'Bit of a long time to keep a secret, Frankie,' he said reproachfully. He knew perfectly well I was lying.

I flushed. 'I want it for myself,' I confessed.

'That's what I thought,' he said, nodding, pleased to be right. 'That's what I told myself. It's Frankie who wants a pet, not her brother. All right. I'll make a hutch for you. How big is this animal?'

'About this size now,' I said, showing him with my hands. 'But it's still growing. Quite a lot.'

'Better make it nice and roomy. Now, we'll have to have wood –'

I told him we'd bring it round this afternoon. I told him we'd help him make it, if he told us what to do, me and John and Julia. I told him we needed it as soon as possible.

'Tomorrow's Sunday,' I said. 'I wondered . . .'

'Yes,' he said, nodding, 'I can come over. Not till the afternoon, mind. Always have Sunday dinner with my mum, see. Mustn't disappoint the old lady. Come over about half past three, right? But what about your dad? Won't he ask what I'm doing coming here on a Sunday?'

'I thought – the back gate?'

He smiled and put his finger against his nose again. 'Secret,' he said. 'That's the way of it, Frankie, Secret.' He thought for a moment. 'Screws, see? Screws are more secret than nails. No hammering. But what about the sawing? Can't get away from that. Have to cut the wood to size. What about that, then?'

'I'll think of something,' I promised.

There were now four of us in the secret. Four was enough. I didn't mean to tell anyone else, but I couldn't help it. Hazel is my best friend, and I could see that she was hurt, though she tried to hide it.

We were carrying the wood when we saw her. It was our third journey. The wood was very heavy and we'd stopped for a rest. I pushed my damp hair back from my sweaty forehead – and there was Hazel, staring at me. She had a towel rolled up under one arm.

'Hazel! Oh Lord, I forgot. I'm sorry. We were going swimming, weren't we?'

'Yes, we were, you cockroach,' she said, but she was smiling. 'Never mind. We can go later. What's all this wood for?'

'Just something we're doing,' Julia said.

'Want a hand? You look as if you could do with some help.'

'No, thank you,' Julia said quickly, before I had a chance to say anything. 'We can manage. Can't we, Frankie?'

I didn't like the way she put her hand on my arm, as if I belonged to her. And I could have done without the satisfied little smile on her face. But I didn't know what to say. I felt myself flushing.

'Suit yourself,' Hazel said, shrugging. She looked at me, 'What about tomorrow? We could go for a swim and then –'

'Frankie's spending the whole day with us tomorrow,' Julia said.

Hazel looked at her, and then at me. I felt terrible.

'I see,' she said, and walked away.

We did pretty well that afternoon. Alf measured and cut the wood, while we cleared and levelled a site for the hutch. I had my transistor going to drown the sound of the saw. John said he thought it improved the sound of the music, and we laughed. I liked John. He and Alf were soon joking about the splendid palace they were going to make for my rare pet, with a four-poster bed and a marble bath. Even Julia smiled once or twice, though she is a serious sort of girl.

It was very hot in the square of ground behind the high hedge. Nobody bothered us. Mrs Drake slept soundly in her deckchair on the terrace. I crept past her once to fetch some lemonade from the fridge, but she didn't wake.

It should have been fun, but I couldn't enjoy it. I kept thinking of the expression on Hazel's face before she walked away. I kept worrying about it. She *is* my best friend.

That evening, when the others had gone to their homes, I went round to see her. I told her everything.

'Of course I can keep a secret, Frankie,' she said indignantly. 'What d'you mean I never do? Oh, at school. That's different. You know what it's like. Someone tells you a secret, then they go straight off and tell it to the next hundred people they meet, so it's hardly worth bothering. But I won't breathe a word about your monster, Frankie, I swear I won't. Cut my throat if I do.'

'I will,' I said.

9

On Sunday Mrs Drake gave us our breakfast and then went off to spend the day with her married daughter at Calmcreek.

'There's cold chicken in the fridge, Frankie, all ready carved,' she told me before she left. 'The salad's washed and just needs the dressing poured on. Then there's that strawberry flan and cream for afters. Think you can manage, dear?'

'Dunno. Sounds terribly complicated.'

My father looked at me, frowning. Mrs Drake smiled.

'Get along with you, dear,' she said. 'Well, if you'll excuse me, I'll be off now and leave you to finish your breakfast in peace.'

The door shut behind her. My father was still looking at me. He takes his duties as a parent like medicine, in small doses at fixed intervals. Sunday morning is his time for us.

'Frances, I don't understand why you found the lunch arrangements complicated,' he said, still worrying about it. 'They sounded perfectly simple to me.'

'It was a joke,' I explained.

'A joke? Oh, I see. You were indulging in irony.'

I smiled uncertainly. There was a slight pause, in which I thought I heard a faint thump overhead. Oh, no!

'Have you two made any plans for today?' my father

asked next.

'I'm going out,' David said quickly. 'I said I was, didn't I? Didn't I tell ycu I was going to be out to lunch, Frankie?'

He hadn't, but I was too pleased about it to argue.

'I expect so. Yes, I believe –' I began. Then suddenly and very loudly I started to sing, 'You told me, you told me, I do believe you told me. One of you is out to lunch, the other's dum-dee daddy.'

They stared at me as if I'd gone mad. I'm usually only noisy at school, not at home. I don't think they had ever heard me sing before, and the experience shattered them.

'What are you making that horrible din for, Frankie?' David asked, putting his fingers in his ears.

I could hardly tell him I was trying to drown out the noise of the monster jumping up and down above our heads. It had grown itself feet during the night, like floppy, upside-down saucers, and although the noise it made was not loud, it was distinctly odd, coming from a room that was supposed to be empty. So I went on singing and beating time on the table with my spoon.

'Frances! Please! That's enough,' my father said, so sharply that I stopped. To my relief, the thumping had stopped too. Monnie must have heard my voice coming through the floor. It was probably hiding under the table again.

'I was only singing. I've got to practise,' I said, for a brilliant idea had just struck me. 'Some of my friends are coming over after lunch, lots of them in fact, and we're going to rehearse our steel band. You know, saucepans and dustbin lids, things like that. I'm to be the lead singer –'

'Good grief,' David said, 'I'd go out if I were you, Dad.'

44

'I suppose I could ask them not to make too much noise,' I said, sounding as doubtful as I could. It worked.

'I've no wish to inhibit your artistic endeavours, Frances,' my father assured me hastily. 'I was thinking I might call on Professor Thompson this afternoon. If you're sure you don't mind?'

'No. That's all right.'

He looked relieved. He doesn't enjoy my company. I don't blame him for that. I don't really enjoy his. When I was little, Aunt Mary looked after me and kept me out of his way, because he's a great scientist and couldn't be expected to deal with small children. So we never got to know one another, and now it's too late. We are worlds apart. He'd never understand how I felt about Monnie. Never in a thousand years.

The sun shone that afternoon. A soft wind made everything in the garden dance, the leaves, the shadows – and me. I was in a silly mood. There are times when life seems to fizz in my veins and I find it difficult to keep still. I was so pleased with myself that even the sight of Julia's sour face seemed of no more importance than a passing cloud.

Only her face didn't pass. It came into our back garden through the door in the wall, and remained like a shadow on my fine day.

I had asked Hazel to come early so that I could show her Monnie before the others arrived, but she was late and they were early. I was waiting outside and I saw them walking towards me, John and Julia from the right, Hazel and Alf from the left. I saw Julia hesitate, and whisper something to her brother, who shrugged.

I had not told Julia that I had told Hazel, and I had not told Hazel that I hadn't told Julia that I had told Hazel. If this sounds a bit complicated – well, it was. They all looked confused and silly, none of them knowing who was supposed to know what. This made me laugh.

'Mustn't make too much noise, Frankie,' Alf warned me. 'Don't want your dad to hear us, do we?'

'It's all right,' I told them happily, jumping up and down. 'I've got rid of him. I drove him out of the house. They're all out. We can make as much noise as we like.'

I told them how clever I'd been and even Julia smiled when she heard, for I'm well known at school for not being able to sing a note in tune.

'Remember when Mrs Perlotti told you in front of the whole class that you sounded like a sick peacock?' she asked.

'That wasn't nice,' Alf said disapprovingly. 'I don't call that nice. I like to hear Frankie sing. People sing when they're happy, don't they? You sing all you want, Frankie. We won't mind. Your teacher had no right to say that.'

He worries about me sometimes. He thinks our house is too quiet. 'You should have your friends round to play, Frankie,' he tells me. I do, but not often. Somehow ours is not a good house to make a noise in. It's dark and its high ceilings echo like a church, so you feel you have to whisper. It's easier to go out.

But this afternoon the house and garden were all ours, and I was happy. The hutch grew quickly under Alf's clever hands, and the hammer rang as we knocked in the posts to hold the wire netting for the run. We laughed and chattered and made a lot of noise. All except Julia.

I didn't know her well enough then to recognise the danger signals; the way her mouth grows smaller when she's angry, and her voice becomes very high and clipped. Even her movements become more precise, as if she's afraid of hitting someone if she lets herself go.

I did not notice at first. She is an easy sort of girl to overlook. Neither pretty nor plain. Very neat. Her hair is fairish and curls naturally. Her dresses are the sort that never crease. Billy Dunbar pushed her into a river at the school picnic. Just for fun, he knew she could swim. She was fully dressed, and I think we all secretly hoped she'd come out looking a mess, but she didn't. Her wet hair merely went into tighter curls and her dress dried with hardly a crinkle. Billy was kept in every night for a week, and his friends blamed her, which wasn't fair. She didn't tell the teachers. I don't know who did, but Julia swore it wasn't her.

I had believed her. I wouldn't have let her into my secret if I'd thought her a tell-tale. But I wished I'd remembered the picnic sooner. Looking at her unsmiling face, I began to feel uneasy.

'What's the matter with Julia?' I asked John.

'Oh, she's a bit miffed.'

'Why?'

He looked at me from under his long, thick fringe, and shrugged.

'Is she sulking because I told Hazel?' I asked.

'Well, you do keep whispering and giggling together. She thinks it's about her. You know what girls are like.'

'It wasn't about her,' I protested. 'Hazel kept asking me to take her up to see Monnie, and I kept saying she'd have to wait. I didn't want Alf to know . . .'

'You mean, you're not going to let him see your monster? After he's made you a hutch for it?' John asked, staring at me. 'I call that downright mean, Frankie.'

'I know it is,' I said unhappily.

The hutch was finished now. It looked beautiful.

'We done a good job, I must say,' Alf said proudly, sitting back on his heels to admire it. 'I hope your pet will be happy in her new home, Frankie. You'll be going up to London for her, I expect. They don't have no rare animals in Jenkin's Pet Stores, only rabbits and hamsters and the like. When are you going to fetch her, then?'

I hesitated. They all looked at me and waited.

I did not want any of them to see Monnie. Not now. Especially not Julia. Monnie was not looking its best today. Apart from that, it had grown again, and I was afraid she would blame me for it.

'Haven't you saved up enough money for her, Frankie?' Alf asked, looking at me so kindly that I felt ashamed.

'Yes,' I said, making up my mind rashly, 'I've already got my pet. I'll bring it down now. I won't be a minute.'

I brought Monnie down in my arms, wrapped up in a big blue towel like a baby in a shawl. It was sleepy and did not wriggle. I kept its head covered as I crossed the upper lawn, so that any nosy neighbours, looking out of their top windows, wouldn't see.

Once safe behind the high, concealing hedge, I set it gently down on the grass, and let the towel fall away.

Somebody gasped and somebody gave a muffled squeal. Then they all stared at it in silence.

Monnie had changed. The jelly-like substance that had given it the semi-transparent look had worn off in patches, or perhaps been absorbed into its body. This gave it an odd, mottled appearance, like a peeling wall. On either side of its head, where its ears should have been, it had grown a vertical fringe of delicate tendrils, like thin green ribbons, covering small slits that opened and shut continually. Its feet were large and floppy and toeless. It had only ten fingers now, but they were all on its right hand. Its crimson eyes were bright.

It sat and stared at us. Then it gazed round at the hutch and the compost heap and the two spindly trees. It was impossible to know what it was thinking.

I looked at Alf. He was shaking his head slowly from side to side.

'I don't know what sort of animal you got there, Frankie,' he said unhappily. 'But I don't like the look of her. I'm sorry but I have to say it. I don't think she's healthy. Not with her skin peeling like that . . . Poor little beggar.' He put out his large gentle hand and stroked Monnie's bald head. 'You're not well, are you? You'll have to take her to the vet, Frankie.'

10

I had a hard time persuading Alf that Monnie didn't
need the vet. He became almost angry with me, which
he'd never been before.

'It's not kind,' he kept saying reproachfully. 'You
got to take her, Frankie. Secrets or no secrets, you've
got to put her health first. I never seen skin so bad
before. Lost all her fur –'

'It never had any fur. It's not meant to. It's not that
sort of animal.'

He looked at me doubtfully, and then back at
Monnie, who was staring intently at his straw hat.
'What sort would you call it, then? There aren't ani-
mals that don't have fur.'

'There are. Frogs, toads, whales, dolphins and – er
– and –'

'Us,' John suggested.

'Don't be silly, John. We're not animals. Besides,
we do have hair,' Julia said, touching her neat curls
complacently. Then she turned to me. 'I think – er –
Alfred is right, though. It's got some disgusting skin
disease. I wonder you can bear to touch it. You'd
better wash your hands with disinfectant.'

'Didn't it look like this before?' Hazel asked.

'No. It was covered with a sort of jelly,' I said. 'Like
frogspawn. It's just wearing off now, that's all. It isn't
ill. Look how bright its eyes are. And it ate all its food,
every scrap.'

Alf was leaning forward, sitting on the ground beside Monnie and peering closely at its skin.

'There aren't any spots or sores, are there?' I demanded.

'No. Can't see none, that's true enough.'

With one finger, he lifted aside the fringe of green tendrils on the side of Monnie's head, so that he could see better the small slits behind.

Monnie made a grab for his straw hat, missed and tumbled over on to Alf's lap.

'Cheeky,' he said, laughing and pushing his hat on to the back of his head, out of reach. Then he turned to me. 'You never said she was a water creature, Frankie. I get it now. They're gills, aren't they? See those slits? She's breathing through 'em. Funny. Never seen that before. Not out of water. What would she be, then?'

'It's – it's a monnie.'

'A monnie? That's a new one to me.' He sounded puzzled but not disbelieving. 'We should've had a pond, Frankie, not a hutch. We should've had a pond for her.'

'No, it's all right. It only starts off in water, then turns into a land animal,' I invented. 'Like a frog.'

For the first time he looked doubtful. 'You having me on, Frankie?'

'I don't mean it *is* a frog, Alf. It's a very rare species. Almost extinct.'

'Comes from the steamy Amazon jungles,' Hazel said obligingly.

'A sort of shell-less swamp turtle,' John contributed.

Julia said nothing.

'Come from abroad, did it?' Alf nodded happily. 'I thought that must be the way of it. You don't get them like that in England. No, Frankie, if you said it'd come from England, I wouldn't've believed you. Even though you're my friend.'

I felt horrible, then. A fine friend I was; a lying, deceitful friend. Alf wasn't stupid. He was good. He trusted me. He never told lies himself. When he sometimes arrived late, he would never make an excuse. He'd just say right out, 'couldn't get myself out of bed this morning. I'll make the time up all right,' and he always did. Here was I, turning him into a figure of fun for my friends to laugh at. I couldn't do it.

'I'm sorry, Alf. It's not true, any of that. I've been lying to you.'

'Have you now, Frankie?'

'Yes. I was afraid to tell you the truth in case –'

'I said I'd keep your secret, Frankie,' he said reproachfully, 'and I would've. I'm good at secrets. You didn't have to tell me lies.'

'I know. Sorry. I won't any more. I'll tell you –'

'Do you think that's wise, Frankie?' Julia said. 'I mean, it's your business, I know, but it won't remain a secret long if you go round telling everybody.' She sounded resentful, as if she thought a secret was like a bag of sweets, and the more I handed it round, the less there'd be left for her.

'Alf's not everybody. And nor is Hazel. They're my friends.'

'And I suppose I'm not?'

'Steady on, Julia,' her brother said, looking embarrassed. 'Frankie didn't say that.'

'Come now,' Alf said kindly. 'We're all friends here.' It was the only silly thing I ever heard him say. He meant well, but it just wasn't true. I disliked Julia. I wished I'd never told her.

'You were going to tell me about the monnie,' Alf went on.

I told him how Monnie came from a complex of buildings on the hill above our town; low, grey buildings surrounded by high wire fences, behind which guard dogs prowled menacingly at night, like wolves. It came from the VAG Laboratories, where my father worked. For the good of mankind. I'm not good at explaining things. I talk too quickly and forget to stop for breath. It's almost as if I was running away from what I'm saying. Alf did not understand.

'This turtle,' he said. 'You mean, they bought it and somebody stole it and give it to you. That's bad, Frankie. That could get you in trouble. Must've cost a pretty penny having her shipped over. What'll happen when they miss her?'

'They won't miss it. It was a tiny blob of jelly when I first got it. No bigger than that.' I held my thumb and forefinger about a centimetre apart. 'It didn't look like an animal then. It didn't even look alive until after the lightning –'

'You overfed it,' Julia said. 'You know you did, Frankie, it's no good trying to blame it on a thunderstorm.'

'Anyway, they won't miss it, Alf,' I said, ignoring her. 'Dav – er – the person who gave it to me said they were only going to get rid of it. It was just waste – you know, the stuff you get left with when you're making something else.' Seeing he still looked puzzled, I added, 'Like . . . oh, like sawdust.'

'Sawdust?' he repeated, looking even more confused.

'We think something must have gone wrong with one of their experiments,' John explained.

'If you ask me, the kindest thing now would be to have it put to sleep.' Julia looked at poor Monnie with distaste. 'It's obviously a mistake.'

'A mistake? You mean, they sent the wrong thing? I get you now,' Alf said. 'Happened to me once. Wrote off for some parrot tulips and what did I get? Daffodils. Didn't throw 'em away, though,' he said, looking rather reproachfully at Julia. 'I planted them. Come up a treat, too.'

53

We gave up then. It was too difficult to explain. Especially as we did not really understand it ourselves. None of us knew what Monnie was, and I had not helped with my talk of frogs and sawdust. No wonder Alf was confused.

He was rather quiet as he put his tools away. I thought he looked worried. We had put Monnie into the run we had made in front of the hutch, and it was standing pressed up against the wire-netting, looking up at us as if to say, 'What have I done? Why have you put me in prison?'

Alf kept glancing at it, and I wondered if he'd guessed the truth at last. Once I heard him mutter, 'A mistake, are you, you poor little beggar? Don't let it get you down. You aren't the only one. We'll see you right. Not going to be easy, mind.'

'How do you mean, Alf?' I asked.

'She's a young 'un, isn't she, Frankie?'

'Yes.'

'Thought so. Has the look of a baby. How big's she going to grow, then?'

'I don't know.'

He nodded, as if this was the answer he expected. 'Have to think of something,' he said.

He was the first to go, as he did not like to leave his old mother alone for too long. Before he went, he offered to keep an eye on Monnie while I was at school, and to give it its meals. 'Won't be no trouble, Frankie,' he said, blushing when I hugged him and thanked him, 'I'm working hereabouts next week and can pop in easily. The back way. Nobody'll notice. She'll be lonely at first. Bound to be. Need a bit of company.'

I stood looking after him as he walked off down the road. Behind me in the garden were my three other helpers. Hazel, my best friend, would be waiting for the others to go, so that we could have a proper talk together, without feeling Julia's suspicious eyes on us

54

all the time. Julia would be determined to prevent this, if she had to stay all night. John – well, John was easier. He would shrug his shoulders and look superior, as if boys were never quarrelsome.

I felt terribly tired suddenly. It was all too much for me. I wished I were small again, and someone big and kind would carry me up to bed, tuck me up and tell me everything was going to be all right. But it was no good. I wasn't a baby any longer. I had responsibilities now.

I turned round and gave them my best party smile.

'Thanks a lot. I don't know what I'd have done without you,' I said, wishing I knew what to do with them now. 'Come up to the house and have some cake,' I said. 'Before you go home. My father will be back soon,' I added slyly, hoping to frighten them away.

After supper, when my father was in his study, Mrs Drake watching television in the sitting room, and David not yet back, I slipped out with a dish of food for Monnie.

It was still standing where we had last seen it, pressed up against the wire-netting, like a prisoner of war on the telly. When it saw me, it started jumping up and down, and whistling softly. It was the first vocal sound I had heard it make. Fortunately it was not very loud.

I let myself into the enclosure and put down the dish, but it would not eat until I sat down beside it. Once, when I tried to get up, it left its food immediately and wrapped its arms round my leg, whistling through the slits on the sides of its head, in a very doleful manner.

When at last it had finished its meal, I put it into the hutch, hoping it would bed down on the clean straw. But it refused to stay there, and in the end I had to sit, holding its hand through the opening, and crooning under my breath a tuneless lullaby. Then it lay quiet. It was too dark now to see if its eyes had silvered over. Twice, when I tried gently to withdraw my hand, it sat bolt upright and began whistling again. It was a very long time before I was able to get away.

11

It was Julia who suggested I should keep a record. She was waiting for us on Monday morning. Usually, though Hazel and I pass the top of her road on our way to school, we don't see her. She leaves earlier than we do. But today she was standing on the corner. She waved when she saw us.

We waved back, Hazel very enthusiastically. Too enthusiastically, I thought.

I had begged her to be nice to Julia, explaining that I could not afford to upset her, in case she turned nasty and gave my secret away. 'I wish I'd never told her,' I said. 'But it's done now.'

'I'll treat her like my best friend,' Hazel promised.

'Don't overdo it,' I said.

I need not have worried. As I have reason to know, Hazel is cheerfully rude to her best friends: she was carefully polite to Julia. I got the impression that they did not like each other very much, if at all.

Julia asked me how my monster was. I told her it had seemed quite happy that morning. When I had taken down its breakfast, I had found it standing in its run, whistling at the birds and flapping its arms up and down. Its skin looked firm and healthy; a dark, smooth grey on its back, fading to a pale silvery green colour in front.

'Has it grown again?' she asked.

'A little. Not much. Hardly at all,' I said shiftily.

'How tall is it now?'

'Um . . . about that.' I held my hand out over the pavement to show her, lowering it hastily when I saw she looked startled.

'Haven't you measured it?' she asked, and looked oddly pleased when I shook my head. 'I expect you've been too busy to think of it,' she said kindly. 'But you ought to make notes every day – height, weight – that sort of thing. Ben will want to know every detail, won't he? You ought to have a record to show him.'

'That's a brilliant idea,' Hazel said. 'You're right. Absolutely right.' I glanced at her warningly. She met my eyes, her face a picture of innocence. Only a picture, not the real thing. Her lips twitched.

Julia had been fumbling in her bag. 'I thought you might like to use this for it,' she said, bringing out a large notebook.

I looked at it in dismay. Anything less like a scientific notebook was hard to imagine. It had a stiff cover, beautifully decorated with birds and butterflies. Its leaves were edged with gold. It was a book for poems and dreams – and the best hand-writing. Mine is not very good.

I did not want to accept such an expensive gift from her. I did not like her. I stammered something about its being too good – any old notebook would do –'

'I want you to have it, Frankie.' Her smile became anxious. There was no way I could refuse it without hurting her. 'Look what I've written inside,' she said.

I opened the book. On the first page, in large, decorated characters, underlined in red and green ink, was written:

THE MONSTER EXPERIMENT

Cold words, I thought. Cold scientific words for a friendly little creature, jumping happily up and down in a sunlit garden, pretending to be a bird.

'Thank you, Julia,' I said at last. 'It's beautiful.' What else could I say?

At ten o'clock that night, I was sitting in my room. On the table in front of me was the notebook Julia had given me, open at the first page. Beneath the elaborate heading, the page was blank.

I wanted to impress Ben. I wanted him to say, 'Frankie, your notes are first class. I'd no idea you had such a keen, scientific brain.'

Some hope. After a year of doing chemistry at school, all that stuck in my mind was this jingle –

Poor Johnny used to drink a lot.

Alas, he drinks no more.

For what he thought was H_2O

Was H_2SO_4.

It did not seem very helpful.

I thought hard.

I must keep my notes short. I must be the cool observer. I must avoid filling the pages with the silly little things that made me love Monnie. The way it would not go to sleep unless I held its hand. The way it watched me when I tried to teach it to count; its eyes, round and puzzled, shining like red currants in the sun. The way it jumped up and down when it saw me coming . . . Ben would only want to know the hard facts.

I picked up my pen and began to write:

THE MONSTER EXPERIMENT

Conducted and observed by Frances Stein

Assistants: Hazel Brent

Alfred Haynes

Julia Hobson

John Hobson

Day One Thursday 8 July.

4.15 pm Obtained M. from unidentified source. It was then small and circular, flesh grey and jelloid, with small dark nucleus in centre.
Diameter: 1 centimetre.
Intake: One teaspoon blood (mine), one pot African violets (mine).
Day Two Friday 9 July.
8 am Height 6 cms. Width 10 cms.
Nucleus has now divided to form two red eyes.
Body humped in middle.
4.30 pm Height and width 30 cms.
Shape square. Appeared dead. Eyes covered by semi-transparent film (later identified as eyelids).
Intake in night: H_2O (one saucer), leaves from rubber plant (mine).
Day Three Saturday 10 July.
Height: 48 cms.
M. now roughly humanoid in shape. No hands, feet, nose or ears. No visible means of breathing. *Query:* absorbs oxygen through jelly coating?
Later in am Grows hands and assorted fingers. This phenonomen observed by Frances Stein, John and Julia Hobson.
In view of rapid growth, M. put on reduced diet. (Four small meals a day.)
Day Four Sunday 11 July.
Height: 54 cms.
During night produced circular feet, and green tendrils on either side of head, in front of small slits through which it appears to breathe.
Jelly-coating worn off or absorbed in patches.
Very active now.
Transferred to hutch at bottom of garden.
Can produce whistling sound through slits.
Nature: Timid and friendly.
NB All measurements given so far are approximate. From now on will be exact.

Apology: Forgot to say that M. eats through sunken mouth in left leg.

Similar mouth in right leg. Purpose unknown. (Perhaps a spare.) Has what appears to be a mouth in face but this, though extremely mobile does not open. Purpose unknown.

Day Five Monday 12 July.

Height: 60 cms.

All jelly coating now gone. M. shows signs of intelligence, eg imitation of birds, affection for Frances Stein.

Appearance: Handsome.

Growth remains rapid in spite of reduced diet. Julia Hobson accuses Frances Stein of overfeeding. Frances Stein denies this.

Hazel Brent confesses she gave M. half a bar of chocolate.

Animal expert Alfred Haynes says he gave it a good dinner and he's not going to starve any animal in his care. He says it's cruel and he's not having it.

Frances Stein, Hazel Brent and John Hobson agree with him.

Julia Hobson

I stopped, and chewed the end of my pen. Julia had cried, but I could hardly put that down. There'd been nothing scientific about her tears. They had been from sheer temper. She had not liked Alf standing up against her, and the rest of us agreeing with him.

Her face had gone pink and her chin began to pucker. We had looked away pretending not to notice, which is the best thing. But John, a typical brother, had said, 'She always blubs when she can't get her own way,' and that, of course, had turned on the tap. We could no longer pretend not to notice, and I had to waste time cheering her up and saying nice things which I'm afraid I did not mean. It's not easy being the leader of a scientific team.

I looked back at the book. 'Julia Hobson . . .' I had written, and what was I going to put now? She would want to see what I had written. After all, she had given me this book. I owed her something, even though I had not wanted to accept it.

I thought; then smiled and wrote: Julia Hobson kindly donated this book for our record, for which we are duly grateful.

There! That should keep her happy.

Before I went to bed, I looked out of the window. The garden was dark and silent. I could hear no sound of whistling in the night.

12

Very early on Tuesday morning, I walked through the sparkling garden carrying Monnie's breakfast. The grass was still wet with dew, the sun shone, a small spider swung lazily on a diamond thread. In the trees, the birds sang morning greetings, but no small creature whistled back.

Monnie was gone. Its hutch was empty. Its run was empty. The rough gate Alf had made hung open.

I had shut it last night. I knew I had. I could remember bending the wire hooks round the post . . .

I searched our garden. It did not take long, being so neat and tidy. 'Monnie! Monnie!' I called softly. It did not come.

I must not panic, I told myself. The garden door is locked. The kitchen door was locked before I opened it. The walls are too high to climb. I mustn't panic, I mustn't, I mustn't . . .

A very old wistaria grows on our west wall. Its thick grey branches loop and intertwine beneath its covering leaves; a baby could climb it safely. From the top of the wall, I looked down into Mrs Pritchard's garden. Unlike ours, it is crowded with bushes and flowers and hiding places. I looked uneasily up at her windows. Mrs Pritchard is old and old people sometimes can't sleep at night. They're glad when it's morning. They get up early.

There was no face at any of the windows. I dropped down into a lavender bush, stepped out of it and looked round. In the middle of the lawn, there was a pond, thick with water lilies. I don't know what made me look there first. Fear, perhaps. I know I was shaking.

I knelt down and parted the round green leaves. At the bottom of the pool, I saw Monnie, lying flat on its back, its wide open eyes staring up through the water. A goldfish swam fearlessly about its head.

I was crying when I lifted Monnie out and laid it on the grass.

It bubbled, whistled wetly, and jumped back into the pond with a great splash, soaking me to the skin. It was only a baby playing games. I had a hard time catching it.

I put it back into its run, gave it its breakfast and tied the gate up with string. It was late when I got back to the kitchen. Mrs Drake was already up. Though she is shortsighted, she is not blind. She blinked at me in astonishment.

'You're wet,' she said.

I told her it had rained during the night, the grass was soaking, I had fallen over and . . . But I did not need any more excuses. The kettle was boiling.

'Run up and change into something dry, dear,' she said, 'while I make us a nice cup of tea.'

We broke up on Wednesday at lunchtime. At first I was glad, because it meant we would have more time to look after Monnie, but soon I was longing for Sunday when Ben would be back from France.

For one thing, David was at home, and though he went out most afternoons with his friends, and slept in late, I could never be quite certain where he was. I had to keep telling my friends not to make too much noise, and they got bored. Also, at breakfast,

I sometimes found my father watching me. I would look up from my scrambled egg, and find his eyes fixed on me, intent, slightly puzzled, as if he were studying something rather odd through a microscope. And I'd wonder if I'd been talking to myself or pulling faces. I'd never noticed his keen interest in me before, and it worried me. I was afraid in case my secret somehow showed on my face.

Every night, however tired I was, I wrote in my scientific notebook before I went to bed. It was hard. My head was a muddle of bright images; the sun beating down on the square of rough grass behind the high hedge, the smell of the compost heap, Monnie playing with the blue ball Hazel had bought it, Julia in a plum-coloured dress being chased by a wasp . . .

Ben would not want to know any of this. Facts, I reminded myself, and sighed. Facts . . .

'How long was it lying at the bottom of the pond?' John had asked.

'Must have been several minutes. I sat on top of the wall, looking round – and even before that I'd been listening carefully for anything moving. I'm sure I would have heard it.'

'Perhaps it's amphibious.'

I must have looked blank, because Julia explained kindly, 'That means it can live both on land or in water.'

'I know that,' I said untruthfully. 'I was just trying to remember how to spell it.'

She told me.

Day Eight I wrote on Thursday.

Height: 76 cms.

There is reason to believe that M. is amphibious.

I turned my head and gazed out at the darkening garden, silent and cooler now, the daisies on the lawn shut tight against the coming night. Behind the high hedge, Monnie slept. I wondered if it dreamed wistfully of the pond next door, with the water lilies and the goldfish. No more escaping now. The gate to its run was padlocked.

'You can't let it get out again,' Julia had said. 'Suppose that poor old lady next door had seen it. She might've had a heart attack.'

She was right. She was always right. It was boring of her.

I grew to dread the sound of her voice, so gloomy and sensible. She hated it when Hazel and I were laughing together. She thought we were too frivolous. I suppose we were.

'Do you realise, Frankie,' she said, 'that if your monster keeps growing at its present rate, it'll be over six foot by the middle of September?'

'It won't. It's slowing down.'

'No, it's not. It grew six centimetres yesterday and five the day before. By your own measurements.'

'Frankie's no good at measuring things,' Hazel said, winking at me, 'She's hopeless. She probably held the ruler upside down. You'd better do it yourself tomorrow, Julia.'

We all looked at her, smiling a little unkindly, and she turned an angry pink. She didn't like Monnie. She'd never touched it, not once. When it came near her, she backed away. I didn't blame her. Spiders made me feel like that. It's something you can't help, like hiccups.

Monnie noticed. After the first day or two, it kept away from her. When Hazel had at last taught it to count its fingers properly – one, two, three, four, five, stop, on each hand – it came to show them proudly to me and John and Alf, but not to Julia.

When its feet changed shape, becoming long and fan-shaped, with five webbed toes on each one, it showed them to the rest of us, but not to her. It did not whistle at her. It did not offer her a bird's feather or dandelion or a bright brown pebble, though it gave its little gifts to us.

'I don't think it likes me,' she said.

'Of course it does,' I lied quickly, to keep her sweet. If you think someone dislikes you, it's only natural to dislike them back all the more, and things were difficult enough already. 'It likes you very much, only it's a bit shy.'

She looked at me. 'I'm not stupid, Frankie,' she said.

There was an awkward little pause, while I tried to think of something to say. Into this silence came four liquid notes, oddly familiar, though at first I could not place them. Someone was whistling over and over again – *dum, dum,* dee *dum* . . .

'That's right,' I heard Hazel say, 'Now the next bit.' She was kneeling in front of Monnie, conducting it with her finger. *'Dum, dum,* dee *dum* dee dee –'

'Stop it!' I shouted at her furiously. 'You idiot, what the hell d'you think you're doing?'

Hazel looked at me in surprise. 'What's wrong? Okay, you may not be a royalist, but there's no need to foam at the mouth just because –'

'Hazel, Mrs Drake's already asked me if I've heard that odd bird that keeps whistling at the bottom of our garden. I told her it was a jay. But I don't think she's going to believe me if it starts whistling 'God save the Queen', do you?'

'Oh! Oh, Lord! Frankie, I'm sorry. I didn't think.' She looked at me with such comical dismay that I couldn't help laughing.

Soon we were all giggling hysterically. Even Julia smiled a little, though she could not resist saying, 'Still, it was a very silly thing to do, Hazel, wasn't it?'

'Yes, it was,' Hazel agreed generously. 'Bone-headed.'

I could have hugged her. I knew she did not like Julia, but was trying not to quarrel with her for my sake. It must have been hard. She's every bit as clever as Julia. It's probably my fault she doesn't get better marks than her at school. I distract her: 'A disruptive influence' Mr Crabtree called me in my school report. It worried my father.

'It only means I talk in class,' I told him.

He looked at me in silence. Then he said slowly, 'You don't talk very much when you're at home, Frances. You're always very quiet.'

'That's what you wanted, isn't it?' I asked.

He looked puzzled. 'I don't understand you, Frances. How do you mean, that's what I wanted?'

'I dunno,' I said, shrugging.

He had forgotten. Well, it wasn't important to him. Years ago, when I was very small and Aunt Mary was still looking after me, I had crept into his study one evening, unnoticed. He was working at his desk, and I sat in the corner watching him. I was curious about this stranger who was my father and whom I hardly ever saw, as I was usually in bed before he came home. I thought he looked old and very sad. I was sorry for him, and wondered if I could make him laugh. People sometimes laughed when I danced and sang and turned somersaults.

But before I had time to try these remedies, Aunt Mary came in looking for me.

'Oh, there she is. I've been searching for her everywhere. I'm sorry, Maurice. I hope she hasn't been a nuisance.'

My father looked up from his work in surprise and then, catching sight of me, said with a smile, 'No, indeed. She's been very good. I didn't even know she was there.'

I expect he meant it kindly, but it had seemed to me then a terrible thing to say. Was that the way to please my father, was that what he wanted? Me to be invisible.

I did not want him to take notice of me now. It was too late. It was the wrong time. I wished he would go away to some conference or other and leave me alone.

Day Nine I wrote, Friday 16 July
Height: 81 cms.

M. still growing rapidly. Alf has had to enlarge door of hutch and remove inner division.

M. keeps standing by wire fence and jumping up and down, its eyes fixed hopefully on the top. We think it needs water. We started digging a pond but the ground is too hard. A bucket of water does not last it any time. It tries to climb into it and knocks it over.

Please come home quickly, Ben. I need your help –

I read these last words with dismay, but there was no way of tearing the page out without it showing. I was tired and I had to get up so early to feed Monnie before anyone was up. Only one more day, and then Ben would be back . . .

On Saturday morning, Ben rang up from France. He and Mike had made some friends who had a villa in Nice. They had been invited to stay on there for a couple of weeks.

'They can't!' I screamed when my father told us. 'They can't! Ben's got to come back tomorrow. He's got to. He said he would.'
I burst out crying, but it didn't do any good, of course. It only made them curious. They couldn't think what was wrong with me.

13

I felt my luck had run out, and this made me nervous.
They were all staring at me.

'Frances, what's the matter?' my father asked.

'Nothing,' I muttered, and left the room before they
could ask me any more questions. Before I shut the
door behind me, I heard Mrs Drake say, 'They promised to bring her a present from France. I expect she's
disappointed that she'll have to wait –'

I wanted to turn round and say that I wasn't a baby
– better not. Why should I care what they thought? I
had more urgent problems.

I was afraid to go down to see Monnie, in case one
of them followed me, so I went up to my room. Once
there, I leaned out of my window and looked down
towards the high hedge. Only the tops of the two
spindly trees showed above it. They were shaking.
Their leaves flapped and shivered, though I could feel
no wind. The air was heavy and still. Oh Lord, what
was Monnie doing now?

Someone knocked at my door.

I moved quickly away from the window. 'Come
in.'

It was David.

'Hello, Frankie,' he said, avoiding my eyes. He went
over to my table and began fiddling with my biro. My
scientific notebook, with its fancy cover, was only an
inch from his hand.

'Leave my things alone!' I said sharply.

He put my biro down and drifted over towards the window.

'What do you want?' I asked.

He turned round, gave me a quick, embarrassed glance and mumbled, 'You lonely or something, Frankie? I mean would you like me to take you to the zoo?'

I couldn't help laughing. The idea so obviously repelled him.

'Who put you up to this?' I asked. 'I bet it was old Drakie.'

'No, it was Dad,' he admitted sheepishly.

'*Dad*? Why? What did he say?'

'Oh, I don't know. He seems to have got some bee in his bonnet . . . You're not worried about anything, are you Frankie? In any sort of trouble?'

'No!'

'Only sometimes it's easier to confide in someone nearer your own age –'

'Like *you*? Is that what Dad told you to say?'

David flushed. 'He might've done . . . Oh, all right, I know we don't get on, but after all, you are my sister. I'd always help you, Frankie, if you were in some sort of fix. You must know that.'

'And then run down and report it all to Dad? No, thank you, David.'

'No!' he said angrily. 'I wouldn't! I wouldn't say a word to Dad if you didn't want me to. What do you take me for? I was just trying to say I'm on your side.'

'Thanks,' I muttered, surprised and touched, for I knew David often found me a pest. I was tempted to tell him about Monnie. Heaven knew I needed help.

But before I could make up my mind, he said moodily, 'If he's so worried, he should've spoken to you himself. Why should I do his dirty work? Come to

71

that, why should I tell him anything? He can hardly be bothered to talk to me.'

Poor David. I'd always thought he and Dad got on quite well. It's true they didn't talk much, but Dad always answered David's questions very patiently. Too patiently, perhaps that was the trouble. No one likes being talked down to.

'I used to wish Professor Blake was our father,' David said. 'He's brilliant, but he never makes you feel a fool. He always sounds interested in what you say ... I suppose he can't be, really,' he added gloomily.

'I don't see why not.'

I knew Professor Blake. I'd often seen him in the park with his two little girls, a large cheerful man, with bright blue eyes and a gingery beard. He liked children. He was always flying kites or playing rounders, or arranging picnics. I, too, had sometimes wished he was our father.

'Dad thinks he's unreliable,' David said. 'Well, not unreliable, exactly, but he doesn't approve of some of his experiments. Of course, Dad's terribly old-fashioned. Bit past it, really. After all, you can't hold back scientific research. You've got to go on, whatever happens.'

'Why?' I asked, looking uneasily out of the window.

David seemed surprised by the question. 'Well, it's progress,' he said vaguely. 'And if you don't do it, someone else will.'

'Do what?'

'I don't think they know exactly themselves yet. That's what makes it so exciting. They've only just begun to see the enormous possibilities. Think of it, Frankie,' he said, his eyes shining with faraway dreams, 'in another ten years, twenty perhaps, we may be able to change everything. Create strange new creatures –'

'What for?' I asked anxiously. The tops of the little trees were motionless now. Perhaps Monnie had gone back to sleep, curled up in a hutch that was now too small for it. 'We can't even look after the animals we've already got,' I added bitterly. 'I shan't have any holiday money left at this rate.'

'What do you mean?'

'Oh, just . . . I gave tenpence to a woman yesterday to save a whale. And tigers are running out . . . What do they want these new creatures for?'

David shrugged. The question did not interest him. 'That's not the concern of the scientists. I expect the politicians will think of something. Use them for food, perhaps, or to control football crowds,' he said.

'You're not going to tell David, then?' Hazel asked.

'And have him fry up Monnie for his supper? No, thank you.'

'He wouldn't! Not seriously, Frankie.'

'No, but . . .' I hesitated. The look on David's face when he had spoken of genetic engineering had somehow put me off. His eyes had been too excited, ambitious, impersonal. I felt he wanted to change the world just to show how clever he was. He was a cold dreamer. I did not think he would care about Monnie the way I did.

I looked at Monnie, who was sitting beside us, playing quietly with some plastic bricks Hazel had brought.

I had got used to its funny face. I knew that when it was happy, its eyes shone, and its mouth moved wildly up and down or into figures-of-eight. When it was sad, as now, its eyes were a dull crimson and its slit mouth rippled a little, like waves on a calm sea. It never cried. I don't think it could. But it whistled softly and mournfully, like a cold wind in the trees.

Poor Monnie. Before going off to mow our lawn, Alf had sawn off the lower branches that overhung its run. It had been trying to escape again. Trying to catch hold of the branches and catapult itself over the wire fence. But it was too heavy. The thin twigs had snapped and the higher branches had remained just out of reach. It must have been trying all morning, for its run was littered with broken twigs. I should not have left it alone so long. But first there had been David and then Mrs Drake had caught me, with similar questions.

'Are you worried about anything, dear?' she'd asked. 'It's not like you to make such a fuss.'

My father had gone off to the laboratories, leaving his spies behind him. They meant well, but I couldn't trust them.

Even my helpers were deserting me. Julia had gone off with her mother to buy some new dresses – well, I didn't miss her. John had gone swimming with his friends, though he had promised to look in on his way back. Alf was here. I could hear him mowing the lawn on the other side of the hedge.

'Got to do it, Frankie,' he'd said. 'Don't want to see a hayfield when I come back, do we?'

'Come back? Come back from where?'

'It's my holiday, Frankie,' he'd said, his blue eyes anxious. 'Going to the Isle of Wight with my brother. Been booked since Christmas. My Auntie Doris is coming in to look after my mum, like she always does. Got our tickets and everything. Tuesday, that's when we're off.' He looked at me unhappily. 'Don't like letting you down, Frankie, but . . . it's all fixed, see? Don't see how I can put it off.'

'Of course you mustn't put it off, Alf. Don't worry. We'll manage.'

'Yeah, but . . . You can't keep her here much longer, Frankie. She's got too big. And if you ask me, she needs to be in water. Look at those feet. Webbed, that's what they are. And that isn't for walking on dry land.'

'We'll think of something. Don't worry,' I said again.

Alf smiled happily, relieved, and went off to mow the lawn on the other side of the hedge. Hazel and I, left alone with Monnie, looked at each other gloomily. We had been trying to think what to do ever since I had told her that Ben was not coming back for another two weeks. We, too, were due to go on holiday soon, first to the seaside with her mum and dad and two small brothers, and then to stay with Aunt Mary in the country. We, too, had been looking forward to it.

'We've got another seven days to think of something,' Hazel said. 'And even if we can't, I'm not going off without you, Frankie. We'll say we want to stay here. We'll manage somehow.'

I smiled at her gratefully, but it was no good. 'Alf's right,' I said. 'Monnie can't remain here, not more than another day or two at the most. I wonder if it could live in the sea –'

'Perhaps we could take it with us, when we go.'

'How?'

She was silent. We both knew it was impossible. Monnie was too big to hide. And we could not expect her parents to help us. They would guess at once where Monnie had come from, and they would be frightened. They'd think it their duty to tell. All the grown-ups I could think of would feel it was their duty to tell. And we were too young. Even David was not yet old enough to drive a car. If only the sea was not so far away . . .

'It needs to be in water,' I said. 'Look how dry and flaky its skin is getting.'

'I'll fill the bucket again,' Hazel said, getting up. 'And I'll ask Alf to fix the sprinkler for us. You know how Monnie likes that.'

Monnie looked up, its eyes shining hopefully. It was very clever. It knew several words now. Often it would stand in front of us, whistling excitedly, the notes going up and down in a pattern like speech. We knew it was talking to us, even though we could not understand what it said.

'What am I going to do with you, Monnie?' I asked now. It looked at me and smiled, and held out a bluey-green brick, the colour of the sea on a fine day. It was just a coincidence. Or a sign from heaven, perhaps.

'But how am I going to get you there? It's too far to walk –'

'Why, David,' Hazel said very loudly, from the other side of the hedge, 'Frankie said you'd gone out.'

'Come and see what I've done with the flowers on the terrace, David,' Alf said, equally loudly, trying to draw him back towards the house.

I picked up Monnie in my arms and looked round wildly, my heart hammering.

'I just wanted to ask Frankie something,' I heard David say. 'She's behind there, isn't she?'

I panicked. I did just about the stupidist thing I could have done. I opened our garden door and rushed out into the street, still holding Monnie in my arms.

14

Two little girls were playing hopscotch on the pavement. They turned round and stared. The youngest, standing on one leg in the middle of a chalked square, wobbled and nearly fell over. But they were not yet frightened, only surprised. I think they thought Monnie was a large, blow-up rubber toy.

Then Monnie turned its head and whistled at them, and their faces changed. Their mouths opened into screaming holes, and they ran off down the pavement as if the devil was after them.

I turned blindly in the other direction and blundered into someone. It was John, coming back after his swim, as he had promised.

'I've got to get away! Where can I hide?' I whispered. I was nearly crying.

Without a word, he took Monnie from me, covered it with his large wet towel so that it looked like a bundle of washing, and began to run down the street. I loved him then. I would have followed him anywhere. He was a true friend.

'Where are we going?' I asked, catching him up.

'My place,' he said briefly. 'They're all out. It'll be – oh, hell!'

We had turned the corner and there were two women coming towards us. Behind us, out of sight, we could hear David calling, 'Frankie! Frankie!' There was no going back. No time to think.

'We'll have to risk it,' John muttered. 'Is anything showing?'

I looked at the bundle in his arms, tucked a webbed foot out of sight – and prayed.

We walked on.

Mustn't run. Mustn't cry or look frightened. Mustn't do anything to draw attention to ourselves. Keep quiet, Monnie. Don't wriggle. Ladies, don't look at us. Go on gossiping together . . . please, keep on talking.

'And I said to her, you can't have it both ways, dear,' the woman in the blue dress was saying as they came up. 'You can't have your cake and eat it, that's what I always say.'

She must have said it too often. The woman in the flowered dress was obviously tired of hearing it. Her attention wandered. She looked straight at us.

'Whatever you got there?' she asked, stopping and staring at the wriggling bundle in John's arms.

'Sick dog. Can't stop. Got to take it to the vet,' he said, trying to get past, but she stood in his way.

'Poor thing, what's the matter with it, then?' she asked, 'should you keep its head covered like that? Might suffocate.'

She stretched out her hand towards the towel. John stepped back quickly on to my toe. I yelped and Monnie whistled loudly.

'That isn't a dog!' the woman exclaimed suspiciously.

'It is! He's swallowed a whistle. We've got to hurry or the vet won't wait,' I cried. *'Please!'*

My tears moved her, and she stepped out of the way immediately. She was a kind woman. 'You run on, dears,' she said. We fled.

'I hope your dog will be all right!' she called after us.

We were round the next corner. At first I thought the street was empty. Then an old man lurched out of a doorway in front of us. In spite of the hot sunlight, he was dressed in a shabby overcoat and had a dirty white scarf wound twice round his neck. His face was red but I thought he seemed cold because he was shaking. He stopped and stared, blinked his pouched, watery eyes, and stared again. Then he crossed himself with trembling fingers and began mumbling something under his breath.

Monnie was struggling in John's arms. Both its long webbed feet were showing beneath the towel, and a hand, with far too many fingers again, tried to pull the covering fold from its head.

'Merciful God . . .' the old man mumbled, staring.

'He's a drunk. They won't believe him,' John muttered. 'Come on.'

We hurried on. Looking back, I saw the old man was gazing after us. I hoped he would not believe it himself, once we were out of sight, and that he would not have nightmares.

We reached John's house, and I held Monnie while he found his key.

'Quick,' he said, and pushed me inside.

He would not let me rest but hustled me down the passage, through the kitchen, pausing only to take a key from a hook on the wall, and then out into the garden.

'For heaven's sake, get it to shut up,' he said.

I patted Monnie gently through the towel, and the shrill whistle gave way to a soft hiccupping sound.

'Where are we going now?' I asked, for we were hurrying down a narrow path between back gardens. The fences were high, but now and then, through a broken plank, I got a glimpse of a little lawn, a line of washing, a red tricycle. I did not feel safe. Monnie was terribly heavy. I held it over my shoulder but it kept wriggling. My arms ached.

'I'm taking you to Dad's yard,' John said.

'Won't there be people there?'

'No. Saturday afternoon,' he said. 'What happened, Frankie? That was David shouting, wasn't it? Has he found out?'

'No.' I told him everything; about my father's choosing the wrong time to start noticing me, how he'd asked David and Mrs Drake to suss me out –

'Why couldn't he ask you himself?'

'I dunno. Doesn't know me well enough, I suppose. Besides, he wanted to go to the lab. He goes every day. He'd live there if there was a bed. I wish he would,' I said. John glanced at me curiously, a little disapprovingly, I thought, and I added hastily, 'I'm only joking. He's not as bad as I make out.'

'He couldn't be, could he?' John said, which silenced me.

I stopped to shift Monnie on to my other shoulder, and lifted the damp towel so that I could see its face. It looked up at me. Its mouth quivered, and then turned up into a smile.

'It won't be long, Monnie,' I whispered. 'We'll soon be safe.'

John was looking at Monnie thoughtfully.

'Frankie, what does your dad do exactly?'

'He's a molecular biologist,' I told him, and hoped he would not ask me what that meant. He did, of course, and I had to confess that I wasn't certain.

'Ben did explain it to me once, but – well, it's a bit complicated,' I said. 'Why?'

'I just wondered. There's an awful lot of talk about what goes on up there . . . You know what people are. I don't suppose half of it's true.'

I bit my lip. The laboratories, squatting on the hill above our town, had cast a shadow over my life that no light could shift. It was no good my father, my brothers and all the people I knew who worked there, telling me the rumours simply weren't true.

They'd say that anyway, wouldn't they? If they had something to hide . . .

'I'm glad my dad doesn't work there,' Debbie Scott had said to me once.

'He's not clever enough,' I'd retorted angrily. 'And they're not doing anything bad. Those dogs and fences, that's just to guard their business secrets –'

'Monkey business!' she'd jeered. 'Bomb business! Bug business! No wonder your dad called you Frankenstein.'

'Don't look so worried, Frankie,' John said now. 'We won't let them get hold of Monnie.' He drew the towel gently over its head again, 'Better keep it hidden. We're nearly there. I'll just go ahead and see if there's anybody about.'

He went on to the end of the lane. I saw him look carefully both ways, and then beckon. When I joined him, I saw we had come out in Kipling Street, and there on the left was his father's yard. There was no one in sight.

John unlocked the padlock, and opened one of the tall wooden gates just wide enough to let me slip through. I waited for him to follow, but he did not come.

'John?' I called softly, suddenly unreasonably frightened.

His face appeared in the gap. It looked worried.

'I can't lock it from the inside, Frankie,' he whispered. 'I don't know what to do. If someone notices the padlock hanging open, they might get curious. Oh damn, I should've brought the other key.'

'What other key?'

'To the back entrance. Look, I'd better lock you in and go back for it. I won't be long.'

'John –'

'Don't worry. The yard's not overlooked. You'll be quite safe.'

81

His face disappeared. The gate shut. I heard the padlock click, and then the faint slap of his trainers on the pavement as he ran off. Then there was silence, except for a doleful whistling.

I put Monnie down and took the towel away. It perked up immediately and looked round with interest. The wet towel had improved the look of its skin, which now gleamed like satin in the sunlight.

There was wood everywhere; planks stacked on long shelves beneath a rusty iron roof, or propped up against the wall at the back. The very air smelled of wood, and there were shavings and sawdust all over the ground.

Monnie had found a large pile of orange sand and was playing in it happily. I sat down on a wooden trestle and watched. First it clambered up to the top, then it rolled over and over to the bottom, until it looked as if it had been coated with bread crumbs. I saw the prints of its webbed feet in the sand, and I thought of the sea.

I thought of mermaids and dolphins leaping and bright, silver fish. I thought of all the room there was in the great oceans for a creature to grow in peace.

But Monnie was so young. How would it manage by itself, without me to bring it four meals a day, and hold its hand when it went to sleep? And I remembered the threatened whales I had given ten pence to save. Was there anywhere left on this planet where a baby would be safe from harm?

'What am I going to do, Monnie?' I said.

It came and leaned against my knee. I felt its sides heaving, going in and out rapidly like a pair of bellows. It was coated with sand. Sand made an orange gash of its slit mouth, and crusted its gills. Frightened it would suffocate, I put out my hand, but before I could brush the sand away, it gave a snort. Puffs of sand billowed out on either side of its

82

head like orange ear-muffs. It did this twice more and then started whistling at me urgently. Once again the notes went up and down in a pattern of speech I could not understand.

'What is it, Monnie?' I asked. 'What's the matter? What do you want?'

It jumped up and down impatiently, pointed at me and then cupped its hands together, lifting its left foot to show me the hidden mouth.

'You're thirsty? You want water?'

It whistled enthusiastically, its eyes shining. I got up, but before I could start searching the yard for a tap, a sudden noise made me swing round. One of the large entrance gates was creaking open.

'John?' I called anxiously.

It was Hazel. She slipped through the narrow gap and the gate closed behind her.

'Hazel!' I cried joyfully, going to meet her.

Then I saw she was crying. 'Oh, Frankie, I'm sorry,' she said. 'It's all gone wrong. Julia's told.'

'Who? David?'

'No. She's told your dad. She's told him everything. We've got to get out of here quick.'

15

There was a door in the high wall at the back of Benson's yard, tucked away behind a wooden shed. It was here Hazel took me, telling me to hurry, hurry –

'Are they coming?' I asked, glancing fearfully over my shoulder. I'm not certain whom I meant by 'they' – the whole of the VAG laboratories, probably, for fear had driven all sense out of my mind. I imagined my father, and all the other scientists in white coats, the guards in their helmets, the dog handlers with their fierce grey shadows, all coming to snatch Monnie out of my arms. Their property. Their experiment. Theirs to do what they liked with.

'Ssh!' Hazel whispered. She had unlocked the door and was peering out cautiously. 'Quick! Over there!'

We came out into a narrow cobbled street or alley, running between Hobson's and the backs of some derelict houses. Their windows were boarded up and their small yards were filled with assorted junk. She pointed at the one directly opposite. It had a large abandoned freezer in its yard, the door and shelves missing; piles of cardboard cartons and some small pieces of rusty machinery that looked as if they belonged in a dungeon. Everything stank of cats. The wall in front was only about two foot high. A child could see over them.

'Can we get into the house?' I asked.

'No. You'll have to duck down behind the freezer if

anyone comes. I'm sorry. It's only till John gets here. Then we'll try and think of something better. I'll keep watch.'

I sat down on an upturned crate, with Monnie on my lap. It must have sensed my fear, for it was trembling. I rocked it gently and it sighed. Its silvery lids began to close. I felt horribly confused.

'It was all Julia's fault,' Hazel whispered from the other side of the low wall. 'I tried not to quarrel with her, Frankie. I tried. But she kept saying beastly things about you. That you were a liar and a cheat and she bet that you'd known all the time that Ben wasn't coming home tomorrow. She said you'd never meant to tell him – you'd only said so to make us help you. And now we were accomplices and could go to prison –'

'That's nonsense! Was David –'

'Hush!'

I waited. I could hear the sound of my heart beating, and cars passing somewhere out of sight.

'False alarm,' she whispered, and went on with her story.

Apparently David had not looked for me very hard. He'd just opened the garden door, shouted once or twice, and getting no reply, had given up. To their surprise, he did not seem curious about the empty hutch. He'd glanced at it, said, 'Good grief, not rabbits. Bet she forgets to feed them,' and gone back into the house. Then John had arrived, with the key to Hobson's back door in one hand, and a huge bag of buns and crisps in the other.

'We were all going to come round to the yard and have a picnic while we decided what to do,' she said. 'It would've been fun. I said I'd get some apples and stuff for Monnie . . . But then *she* came and spoiled it all. I'm glad I tore her new dress! I'm glad!'

'Hush,' I said anxiously, for her voice was rising.

'Sorry,' she whispered, glancing quickly up and down the alley. 'Where was I?'

'You'd torn her new dress.'

'It was a stupid dress. I suppose she was cross because we didn't all go into raptures when we saw it. We didn't even notice. We were busy telling her what had happened. That's when she started. She said we were stupid. She said Monnie was dangerous and she didn't want it hiding in her dad's yard. She said it was our duty to tell someone, and if we wouldn't, she would. She'd tell David. That's when I tore her dress. I didn't mean to, I was just trying to hold her back. She screeched and pushed me into John and we fell over. And she got away. She went running towards the house, with Alf after her, shouting at her to come back. We'd got up by then and we came out from behind the hedge and – oh, Frankie, your dad was on the terrace. And she was telling him! She was telling him all about Monnie! We heard her!'

'Oh, no!' I whispered, holding Monnie tight. 'Oh, no!'

'We didn't know what to do. Then John gave me the key and whispered I was to get you out the back way and wait for him here.'

'What's he doing?'

'He said he'd tell your dad we were only playing a monster game, and Julia got frightened. He'll say we played a trick on her and the silly girl believed us. Alf promised to back – Get out of sight!' she hissed suddenly, staring at something I could not see.

Holding Monnie, I crept behind the freezer and crouched down. Monnie stirred, and slept on.

There was the sound of something rattling over the cobbles, a brake squeaked, and then silence. I waited, trembling. Now more noises – voices saying something I could not hear, an odd creaking, followed by a loud clang. Then the sound of footsteps going away.

'It's just a truck delivering something to that flower shop at the end,' Hazel whispered. 'I don't think it'll be staying long. I heard the driver say it was her last trip, thank heaven. She'll be glad to get home.'

'She? You mean, it's a woman driver?'

'Yeah. No one I know. One of those country types – you know, with wellies and muddy trousers. That sort.'

I came out from behind the freezer to have a look. It was an open truck, parked a few yards away and completely blocking the alley.

'Hold Monnie a minute,' I said, and went up to the truck. The back was empty, except for some old sacks, a coil of rope, a scattering of leaves and earth, and a crumpled tarpaulin, thrown carelessly over half the floor. On the side of the truck was painted: Didon Nurseries, Swaley Lane, Didon.

I climbed into the back, and pulled the tarpaulin towards me.

'Frankie! What are you doing?' Hazel whispered anxiously, coming up.

'Give me Monnie,' I said, leaning over the tailboard and holding out my arms.

'No! You can't – it's too risky. I won't let you.'

'Quick! Give me Monnie,' I said again, almost crying now. 'Please, Hazel, *please.*'

She hesitated, then lifted Monnie up to me. 'I'm coming too.'

'No. I need you to cover for me,' I said, putting Monnie down carefully on a bed of old sacks. It opened its eyes and blinked at me. Then it shut them again. 'Find David. Tell him – oh, you'd better tell him the truth. Say I'll never forgive him if he lets me down. He promised, he promised he wouldn't give me away. Can you do that?'

'I'll try,' she said, looking worried. 'But what about you?'

'Tell them I've gone to the pictures. Tell them anything – I won't be long. I'll just take Monnie somewhere safe, then I'll come back by bus.'

'Where are you going?'

'Where the truck takes me,' I said.

It was not that I didn't trust her. But everyone knew that she was my best friend. If I was late back, she would be the first person they'd ask. They'd go on and on at her until her head spun, and she'd begin to wonder if she ought to tell, for my sake. I just wanted to save her a headache.

'But Frankie –' She began, then broke off. A door had opened and we could hear two women talking. 'See you on Wednesday,' one of them said. Hazel backed silently into the shadow of the wall. I lay down and lifted the tarpaulin over me and Monnie.

I heard heavy footsteps, the cab door opening –

Monnie stirred, tried to sit up and whistled loudly.

'Who's that?' the woman called.

I put my hands over Monnie's gills and felt its breath warm on the palms of my hands. It kept quiet.

'Who's there? It's no good hiding. I heard you,' the woman said, and I heard the thump of her feet as she jumped down from the cab.

'It was only me,' Hazel said. 'Sorry if I made you jump. You haven't see a small white dog anywhere, have you?'

'Sorry. You'd better check under my truck. I nearly lost a cat that way. Silly creature had gone to sleep. Not there? Well, I must be off. Hope you find it all right.'

The truck shook, the cab door slammed, and the engine started. We were on our way. As we drove out of the alley, I lifted the edge of the tarpaulin and peered cautiously over the tailboard. Hazel was standing and gazing after us, looking as small and lonely as I felt. I wished I had let her come with me after all. But it would not have been fair. Her mum and dad would have been worried sick if she was late back. Not that I meant to be late myself, but you never can tell what will happen, can you?

16

The truck rattled along slowly, stopping and starting, turning left and right and left again, until I lost all sense of direction. I was afraid to lift the tarpaulin and look out. I could hear traffic. We must still be in the town.

I began to feel uneasy. Perhaps the woman was not going back to Didon after all. 'I'll be glad to get home,' she'd said. For all I knew, her home was in another village, miles away. The more I thought about it, the more likely it seemed. Who would choose to live in Didon if they didn't have to?

Didon is small and ugly, a mere straggle of grey houses. Most people drive straight through it on their way to the sea. They pass the lane to Mendicote without noticing it. It has no signpost.

Mendicote is not a show place. It is only a big old house of no interest to anybody but me. And even I did not want to see the house itself – nor be seen by the people who lived in it. I just wanted to trespass on their land, to climb a gate marked PRIVATE, and make my way down through the tangled woods to Didon Creek.

Aunt Mary had taken me there, one hot summer long ago. She had frowned at the sign marked PRIVATE, shrugged, and helped me climb the gate. 'Don't see why we can't swim in the creek,' she'd said. 'The sea doesn't belong to anyone, or if it does, it shouldn't. It should be free for all.'

Free for Monnie – a quiet stretch of blue water, hidden by thick green woods. A private place, a secret place. The woods were overgrown and steep, filled with the sound of water rattling down to the sea. The path, if there had ever been one, was lost beneath dead leaves and brambles and fallen branches. We hadn't met anyone.

People must have gone there once. There was an old summer house overlooking the creek, where we'd once sheltered from the rain. It couldn't have been used for years. There were spiders in every webbed corner, and weeds growing up through the floor, and the windows were cracked.

A home for Monnie. I would make a bed out of dead leaves and soft ferns, gather tender green plants for its supper, and fresh water from one of the noisy streams that splashed through the trees. Tomorrow I could come back with Hazel, and we would teach it to swim in the creek, and catch fish for itself. Tonight I would have to shut the door.

Poor Monnie. I hoped it wouldn't be frightened, alone in a strange place, with the sounds of the night-time woods all around, the creaking and the whispering, and the hooting of owls. I couldn't stay with it. I had to catch the bus home . . .

Home, I sighed, remembering what was waiting for me. Trouble. It was no good John's telling my father that we had just been playing a silly monster game. Some men might have believed him, but not my father. He worked at the laboratories. He knew what they were doing up there, behind the high wire fences. He knew what he had done himself – and he'd want Monnie back.

Never, I thought, I'll never give Monnie up.

He'd be terribly angry with me.

91

The truck was bouncing along at high speed now, making me shake. I wasn't trembling. There was no reason why I should be frightened of my father. He was nothing like the mad scientists in old horror films, with glaring eyes, and a nasty habit of drinking from smoking beakers and turning into monsters while you watched.

No. He was a quiet, respectable man, not given to strong drink. Very neat and clean and methodical. He had never hit me or shouted at me. He spoke to me kindly and patiently when he noticed I was there, and was always careful to remember my birthdays. I don't like dolls, never have, but you couldn't expect him to know that. He has more important things on his mind. Like making monsters.

I'd never seen him lose his temper.

Oh well, it'll be interesting, I told myself. Instructive. I wonder if he turns red or white with anger . . .

Perhaps I should run away. Stay with Monnie in the green woods, live off berries and things. Wrong time of year for blackberries . . . Well then, steal carrots and lettuces from cottage gardens, suck milk from the cows – Yuk! I wanted my tea and buttered toast and jam. I was hungry already.

Oh well, never mind.

The truck suddenly swerved to the left, swung round in a half circle and stopped. The sound of the engine died away. We were there, wherever that might be. I held my breath. The cab door opened and slammed shut. Footsteps on gravel came towards the back of the truck . . . passed on . . . died away. Somewhere in the distance a door shut.

I lay motionless, listening. I could hear a plane buzzing high above. I could hear Monnie snoring gently. I could hear my heart beat.

Cautiously, I lifted the edge of the tarpaulin. Sunlight surprised me, dazzlingly bright. I blinked and looked round. The truck was parked by a rough stone wall. Looking the other way, I saw rows and rows of little trees, standing in line, each wearing a bright orange label. Through their broomstick trunks, I could see splashes of bright colour, reds and yellows and purple. Didon Nurseries. We were here, in the right place. It was only half past five and the sun shone.

So near . . . Must be careful . . . I could not see the building, but it must be here somewhere, perhaps behind that high trellis.

I woke Monnie gently, and wrapped it in a sack. It blinked up at me, still half-asleep.

'Hush,' I whispered warningly. 'Keep quiet, Monnie.'

I lowered myself carefully to the ground. Even so, the gravel seemed to roar under my feet. Now, Monnie –

My luck had changed. No one shouted. Only a solitary blackbird saw us climb the wall. It burst into its staccato warning, but nobody took any notice of it. Even the other birds were not interested in us.

We crossed a patch of rough ground, and climbed a stile. Now we were in a small meadow, enclosed by high hedges. It was wide open to the sky, yet somehow it felt safe. Nine black and white cows grazed peacefully on the far side. One of them raised its head and stared at us with mild curiosity for a moment, then went on eating. We were accepted.

We stood hand in hand, looking round. It was a pretty place. The grass was studded with buttercups, and hazed with meadowsweet and patches of white clover. Honeysuckle crowned the hedges, and at their feet, foxgloves grew and tufted vetch and blue scabious. A small stream pushed its way lazily through the grass.

Monnie stood still, and gazed around with wide-open eyes. Then it looked up at me. Its eyes shone with delight, and it smiled. I think it thought it was in paradise. I almost thought so, too. The evening sun was so golden and the air so sweet. Nothing, I felt, could possibly go wrong now. Not here.

Which just shows how mistaken I can be. After all, things went wrong in paradise, didn't they?

17

I should have had more sense. I shouldn't have let the false enchantment of the summer evening take me in. But I couldn't help it.

Miss Tapier at school once told me I was too volatile. I'd looked it up in the dictionary.

'I'm not!' I'd protested indignantly. She looked round, 'You again, Frankie? What is it now?'

I pointed – "Volatile: capable of being vaporized at a relatively low temperature."

She read it over my shoulder, and laughed. 'I should've remembered I was talking to the daughter of a scientist,' she said, and pointed further on. I saw there was another definition: "Liable to sudden changes of mood."

She was right. I am apt to go up and down.

I had been down. Down at the bottom of a truck, with a black cover over my head, heavy and smelling of earth, like a grave. I was tired of being frightened. I'd been frightened too long. I needed a change.

Monnie was so happy. It wanted to explore everything, touch everything, taste everything. It rolled in the grass, jumped over the tussocks and paddled in the stream. The cows ambled over and mooed at it softly, and it chirrupped with delight. We had taught it to trust us, and it showed no fear of this new world. There were so many things to see and do. We idled along as if we had all the time there was, and nothing to worry us.

I should have remembered that people live in the country, that we might meet someone round any corner, a farmer or a woman walking her dog. But Monnie's joy infected me. I felt lucky. I thought my luck would last for ever.

We had been following the stream, for I was sure it must be going to Didon Creek. But in the third field we came to, it suddenly ran into a bank and disappeared through some sort of dark grating. This was the last we saw of it.

'Where now, Monnie?' I asked.

It whistled sleepily, and held up its arms, wanting to be carried. It was tired now, not being used to walking so far on its short, fat legs.

'No. You're too heavy,' I told it, shaking my head. 'We must be nearly there. If only I could see . . .'

There was a thick hawthorn hedge on the top of the bank. I jumped up and down, trying to see over it, but it was too high, and I couldn't see a gap. Somewhere behind it, the woods of Mendicote were hidden, but which way? I sighed. It was a very long hedge.

I looked round. Monnie was lying in the shade of a big tree. Fast asleep.

'It's all very well for you,' I muttered. 'I'm tired, too. Didn't think of that, did you?'

I leaned against the tree. Looked up at it. It was an enormous old oak, its branches spreading down towards the ground. An easy climb. I glanced at Monnie once more. It was lying on its back, almost hidden by the long grass. Its eyes were shut. I looked up at the tree again.

Good view from the top, I thought.

I like climbing trees. I went up and up through the branches, higher than I needed to go to see over the hedge. I was enjoying myself. When the branches thinned out and began to bend under my weight,

96

I looped my arm round the trunk and leaned out sideways. Through a gap in the leaves, I saw the enclosed woods of Mendicote. I could even see the gate leading into them, no more than a few yards away on the other side of the hedge –

Monnie whistled frantically. A shrill, piercing sound, full of terror. I heard voices shouting. I could see nothing below me through the crowding leaves.

I came down dangerously fast, slithering and bumping through the branches, grazing my face and hands as I tried to stop myself falling. I hit the ground so hard that all the breath was forced out of my body. As I doubled up, gasping for air, I could still hear the desperate, high-pitched whistling ringing in my ears.

The boys did not notice me. They were standing in a circle round Monnie, yelling at it, their faces contorted with hate and fear. Many of them had sticks in their hands, and as I staggered to my feet, I saw one of them throw a stone.

It hit Monnie on the head, and the poor creature winced, looking round in a bewildered way and putting its hands up helplessly against the stones that followed. The tallest boy raised his heavy stick –

'No! Stop it! Stop it!' I screamed hoarsely, and ran towards them, stumbling over the bumpy grass.

A boy caught my arm and tried to hold me back, shouting something. I hit him hard, and pulled away. Another boy put out his foot and tripped me before I could reach Monnie. I fell flat on my face. By the time I'd picked myself up again, Monnie had gone.

The boys were still there. At first there seemed to be hundreds of them, but I suppose there were only about a dozen. They were all staring at me.

'Where's Monnie? Where's it gone?' I shouted. 'What've you done with it?'

They backed away from me uneasily. Some of them were quite big, older than I was, but they seemed almost afraid of me. Perhaps they thought I was mad. I suppose I looked wild enough, with blood on my face and arms, and leaves tangled in my hair.

'Which way did it go?' I screamed.

'You let it alone,' a boy muttered sulkily. 'It could hurt you. It could kill you easily. Never seen anything like it. Horrible.'

'It was a monster,' a small boy said. 'It was going for us. We had to chase it off.'

'We ought to fetch the dogs,' a third said. 'We ought to set the dogs on it. It's dangerous, a thing like that.'

'It isn't! It isn't dangerous! I'll kill you if you've hurt it!'

They muttered together, eyeing me doubtfully.

'Is it yours?' one of them asked.

'Yes. Where did it go? Did any of you see where it went?'

'What is it, then?'

'A baby. It's only a baby,' I shouted. 'You'll go to prison. You'll go to prison if it dies. Where did it go?'

They started arguing together in low voices, looking at me over their shoulders, edging away.

Where did it go?' I screamed at them.

They started running, racing away from me over the grass. I called after them, telling them to come back, but they took no notice.

'I didn't do nothing,' a voice said behind me. 'I wasn't one of them.'

I turned and saw a small boy staring at me. He was no more than five or six, a stocky child with fair hair and a dirty face.

I drew in a deep breath and tried to calm myself. 'Did you see where Monnie went?' I asked gently.

'Monnie? Is that 'er name?'

'Yes.'

'Funny name,' he said. 'Is it short for Monica?'

'Yes. Did you see which way she went?'

'I got a cousin called Monica.'

'Have you?' I wanted to scream. I wanted to shake him, but it wouldn't have done any good. 'Please, it's very important. Did you see where Monnie went?' I asked again.

'I saw 'er,' the small boy said. 'She ran right past me. But I never touched 'er.'

'No, I'm sure you didn't. *Where did she go?*'

'Into the woods,' he said, pointing to the left. 'I'll show you.' He took my hand and looked up at me curiously. 'You're crying,' he said, and led me to a concealed gap in the hedge some yards away. We came out on to a lane and he pointed again. 'There. See the trees. Them's Mendicote woods. Private. I saw 'er go under that gate. Tight fit it was, but she done it quick – pop!'

I raced towards the gate without even thanking him. As I ran, I could hear him pounding after me.

'I'll 'elp you!' he shouted.

I climbed the gate and paused, looking back.

'I'll 'elp you,' he panted. 'I'll 'elp you.'

'No. You'd only frighten her.'

'I never 'urt 'er. It wasn't me.'

'I know,' I said quickly. He smiled at me so hopefully that I hesitated. Then I shook my head. 'No. Thanks, but you'd better go home. Go on, now. Off with you.'

He walked away slowly, dragging his feet, a small, disappointed figure. I turned away and forgot him.

'Monnie! Monnie!' I called, going down into the woods, looking from side to side, searching.

I heard rustling in the undergrowth, whistling in the trees, but it was only the woods mocking me. I did not find Monnie. I blundered on, through bushes

99

and brambles, with the sound of water always in my ears. At last I came to the creek, lying still and quiet and golden in the dark rocks. Ripples ran gently across its surface, moving towards the sea. The tide was going out. I could not see Monnie anywhere.

18

There was no small figure on the rocks. The summer house was empty, the dust and cobwebs undisturbed.

I searched the woods again, calling, 'Monnie! Monnie! Monnie!'

No one answered. The birds were silent now. It was dark under the trees. I tripped over hidden roots. Holly pricked me. Brambles caught at my legs. Something brushed my face and was gone. Here and there, on the dark ground, cold, green goblin lights glowed faintly. Fox fire. It made me think of witches and will-'o-the-wisps, things I was too old to believe in. But not now, not here. The woods frightened me. They kept whispering.

All round me, bushes stirred and rustled. I began to be afraid of what I might find behind them. 'Monnie? Monnie?' I called doubtfully. Silence. And then the rustling began again.

Now it was too dark to see anything. Painfully I made my way back through the whipping branches, following the sound of the streams. Once out of the wood it was still light. The sun was sitting on the tops of the trees on the other side of the creek. Shadows crept towards me, but there was still sunlight on the nearby rocks, and the water beneath them was the colour of cider.

I began searching the rocks again, going further out towards the sea. My scratches and grazes burned, and

101

I had cut my knee quite badly. My legs kept slipping and stumbling. I caught my foot in something and fell forwards on to a flat rock. And there, right below my nose, I saw a few grains of bright orange sand. Builder's sand. Monnie had been here.

It was near the edge of the rock. I stared down into the water anxiously. It was as clear as glass, and I could see the stones on the bottom. Nothing else.

'Monnie! Monnie!' I called. My voice rang out over the quiet water, and the echo came coldly back, 'Monnie! Monnie!'

I took off my skirt and, jumping down into the creek, began swimming round in circles, trying to see if there was anything lying on the bottom. But it was deeper here, and thick with green shadows. Once I saw a dark shape below me and dived down, but it was only weed.

I swam further out, stopping every now and then to tread water and call again. There was no answer. The sun went down beneath the trees, and the moon came up. I was cold now. My arms and legs were so heavy. I could hardly move them. There was a sharp pain in my side. Frightened, I looked back towards the rocks. I had come out too far.

I couldn't get back . . . I couldn't . . . The water kept washing over my face, filling my mouth, my lungs . . . It was too far.

Something came up beneath me and buffeted me forwards.

I dreamed I was lying on a hard bed. I must have been ill, because I kept coughing and wanting to be sick. Although it was dark, I could hear a bird singing. They've drawn the curtains, I thought. Someone was stroking my hair back from my face with a cool, wet hand. Someone was looking after me. Strangely, I felt happy. I was sorry when I woke up.

I could not think where I was at first, and I was frightened. I hurt all over when I moved, and I was soaking wet. Then I turned my head and saw a stretch of dull grey water beneath a dull grey sky. It was raining.

I remembered then. I sat up, wincing, and looked at the dark, dripping woods and the empty grey water, and I was still frightened. I thought of Monnie and wanted to cry.

My wet skirt was lying over my legs and I put it on. I had no idea of the time. Somewhere in my long search, I had lost my watch. I thought it must be nearly morning, though there was no pink in the sky, and the birds were quiet.

I wondered what my father was doing, and David and my friends. I felt terrible. Perhaps I was going to die. They couldn't be cross with me then.

It was silly to sit out in the rain, shivering. I began to push myself up. Then I saw the flowers, pale and delicate, their stems tied with grass. I took them in my hand and stared at them. I remembered my dream, if it was indeed a dream; the soft whistling in the dark, and the wet hand stroking the hair back from my face. I remembered something buffeting me through the water, again and again, until my fingers had touched rock.

'Monnie!' I cried joyfully.

But Monnie had gone. A trail of small pebbles and wet leaves ran down to the water's edge, and I saw one or two leaves floating out to sea. It had left a message for me, and gone off to find a new world for itself, where no one would hate it because it was different.

'Good luck, Monnie,' I whispered.

They came for me an hour later. Voices shouting in the dark woods. Lights flaring yellow between the

103

trees. I came out of the summer house and stood waiting for them.

The voices came nearer. The torches burned like yellow eyes hunting for me. It was still dark in the woods, though the sky was much lighter now and it had stopped raining.

'Frances! Frances! Frances!'

It was my father's voice. It sounded hoarse, as if he had been calling for me all night. I don't know why I didn't answer. I just stood there stupidly until he came out of the trees. Then, when I saw his face, I ran towards him and he took me into his arms.

'Oh, thank God, thank God,' he said, over and over again.

His eyes were red as if he had been crying, and his hair was in a right mess, but he didn't seem to care. He was so glad he had found me at last.

There were other people there, talking, crowding round. Somebody asked me if I had been attacked. I shook my head. My father would not let them ask me any more questions.

'Later,' he said.

I remember vaguely being carried up through the woods, and put into the car. I must have slept then, for the next thing I remember clearly was lying in bed and Mrs Drake trying to get me to drink something. I didn't want it and I pushed her hand away.

'Come on now, Frankie. No nonsense,' Dr Jenkins said, taking her place. 'Get this down, there's a good girl. It'll make you sleep.'

It did. I slept for nearly twelve hours without dreaming.

19

The first time I woke it was evening. My father was sitting on the chair by my bed. He looked tired, but when he saw my eyes were open, he smiled. His questions were all kind ones, and easy to answer – how did I feel? Was I warm enough? Could I manage a little hot broth?

I was still weak and a bit weepy. I drank half a cupful of chicken broth, and then turned my head away fretfully. On the table beside my bed, I saw a bowl of fat red roses.

'Where are the wild ones?' I asked, looking round the room anxiously. 'I had them. I was holding them in my hand. Where've they gone? I haven't lost them, have I?'

My father looked puzzled. He put his hand gently on my forehead. His skin felt warm and dry and a little rough. Nothing like the cool, wet hand that had comforted me in the night. That had left its gift of flowers on the rock beside me, its last gift and I had lost it. I turned my face into my pillow and wept.

I must have gone to sleep again, for when I next opened my eyes, daylight was streaming through my curtains, and there was nobody in my room. I sat up. There were several get well cards on the table by my bed. Their good wishes had come true too quickly. My scratches had scabbed over. My bruises no longer hurt unless I pressed them. The cut on my knee was covered by a neat plaster. I had recovered, and I wasn't at all sure that was what I wanted.

There would be difficult questions now, and I did not have any answers ready. I had no idea what had been happening while I slept. I did not want to have to think and plan. Birds kept whistling in the empty garden. Monnie was gone. All I wanted to do was cry, but you can't go on crying for ever.

I began sorting through the get well cards, comforted by the number of my friends. The one from Julia I threw away as if it burned my fingers. The ones from Hazel and John and Alf I put on one side. I knew they were trying to tell me something, but my brain felt sluggish and sad.

I read them again.

The one from Hazel said: 'Dear Frankie, Came round but you were asleep. I am sorry. It was a stupid game. See you tomorrow. Love Hazel. P.S. Sorry. I had to tell your dad you'd gone off in the Didon nursery truck when you didn't come back.'

I looked at John's card: 'Dear Frankie, Hope you are better soon. Sorry about my practical joke, but I never thought you girls would take it seriously. See you soon, love from John.

Alf's card was more cryptic: 'Dear Frankie, Get better. Your dad says you can have that rabbit I told him about, you know, the one we made the hutch for –'

The word 'rabbit' was underlined. Looking back at the other two cards, I saw that 'game' and 'practical joke' were written in slightly darker ink so that they stood out from the other words. Game . . . practical joke . . . rabbit. That was the message. My friends were still covering for me.

I lay back and thought about the complicated lies I would have to tell, and wondered if I'd get away with them. I knew too little. 'Game' and 'practical joke' were easy enough, but how did the rabbit fit in? Surely they can't have said that I had gone off to Mendicote woods to try and catch one? Nobody would believe that. My head ached.

The questions I dreaded were strangely slow in coming.

David and Mrs Drake were the first people to arrive, bringing me breakfast in bed. Neither of them asked me why I had run away to Didon creek. Mrs Drake fussed round me, plumping up my pillows, and telling me to eat everything up, there's a good girl.

'Now you're not to worry, dear,' she said. 'Your dad will explain it all. It's wicked the things they say, frightening you children. And not a word of truth in it, as I could've told you . . .'

I could not understand what she was talking about.

'As if your dear father would lend himself to anything like that,' she said as she left the room.

I looked at David.

'I suppose it's all my fault,' he muttered, cracking open my egg for me. 'I mean, I've heard the talk, who hasn't? But I never thought you'd believe . . . Why didn't you ask me, Frankie, instead of working yourself up into such a state? You weren't really going to chuck yourself in, were you?'

I began to feel that I must have slept longer than I thought, and like Rip van Winkle, had woken into a world I could no longer understand.

'What day is it?' I asked.

'Monday. Frankie, are you sure you feel all right now?'

'Yes.'

He looked worried and, cutting my bread and butter into fingers, told me to eat up. 'I expect Dad will be coming up soon,' he said. 'I heard him ring up the lab and tell them he wouldn't be in today . . . Frankie, are you well enough to talk? Only I wondered . . . You know that stuff I took? You haven't been worrying in case we got into trouble about it, have you? Not that *you* would. It was me who took it. They couldn't blame you. Besides, Professor Blake hasn't even missed it –'

'Professor Blake?' I asked, feeling more confused than ever.

'You know him. Big man with a ginger beard. We were talking about him only yesterday.'

'Of course I know him. But what's he got to do with it?'

'That stuff I took from his lab – I gave you a bit. Don't you remember anything about it? It wasn't that, then,' he said, looking relieved. 'I was afraid you might've been worrying in case they found out.'

'No.'

So Monnie had come from Professor Blake's laboratory, not our father's. I wished I could think more clearly. David had said something about his experiments – what was it?

'I can't remember,' I said fretfully.

'Don't worry about it,' David said, looking at me with concern. 'You haven't got a headache, have you? I'd better go. I don't want to tire you out. Dad will be coming up soon.

My father came up at ten o'clock. He asked me how I was feeling, and looked pleased when I said I was better. He told me Dr Jenkins would be coming in again before lunch, and that all my friends were anxious to see me, when I felt up to it.

'I'd like to see them,' I said.

'I think they want to apologise,' he said. 'They didn't realise it would upset you so much. They've been terribly worried about you. We all have.'

108

'Sorry,' I mumbled.

He stood by my window for a moment, looking out. Then he came and sat down by my bed. Now, I thought unhappily, now the difficult questions will come. I wasn't ready for them!

'Frances, don't look so alarmed,' he said quickly. 'I'm not going to scold you. I blame myself. I blame myself entirely. I should have realised how unhappy you were.'

I did not know what to say. Unhappy? I thought of the sun shining on the rough grass behind the high hedge; of Alf and John laughing together. Hazel teaching Monnie to whistle 'God Save the Queen,' Monnie proudly showing me its fingers, five on each hand at last . . . I had not been unhappy then. I was unhappy now.

'Sometimes it helps to talk to someone,' my father was saying. 'I know it isn't always easy. But things can grow out of all proportion if you keep them to yourself –'

Like Monnie? I thought, biting back a nervous desire to laugh. It had certainly grown out of all proportion. But he did not mean Monnie, of course. He was talking about the secret fears and worries children have, and never tell anyone about.

'I was just the same,' he said. 'I never found it easy to talk to my parents. I used to think that when I had children, I'd manage better, but – I haven't, have I? I'm sorry, Frances.'

I felt embarrassed. I knew I ought to fling my arms around his neck and tell him he was a splendid father, but it was no good. It's the sort of thing you have to do without thinking, or not at all. Otherwise, it doesn't ring true.

I mumbled something. I don't know what.

There was an awkward silence, then he said gently, 'Can't you tell me about it, Frances? I want to help.'

Game ... practical joke ... rabbit, I thought in confusion. But I did not want to lie to my father now. I felt it would spoil something between us that was just beginning. A sort of warmth. But how could I tell him the truth?

I looked down at my hands and did not say anything.

I thought he would go then, disappointed. But though he got up from the chair and walked round the room, he did not leave. Instead he started talking about the VAG laboratories.

They were financed by an international company, he told me. A few scientists, like himself, were doing pure research; others were concerned with putting their findings to a practical use, in new fuels, medicines, improved crops and livestock.

They were not in any way connected with germ warfare, atomic bombs, or any other weapons whatsoever, he assured me. The rumours going round the town were utterly untrue.

'I suppose you heard them at school, Frances?'

'Yes.'

'I'm sorry. I should have realised how much it would worry you. I ought to have explained ... How much do you know about my work, Frances?'

I did not answer. I always hated having to confess ignorance. I suppose I was more like David than I thought.

'I'm a molecular biologist,' he said. 'I work with Professor Hudson and Dr Clarke, who are both botanists. There's nothing frightening or, indeed, very new about what we are doing ...'

He began talking about genetic engineering, trying to explain it simply so that I could understand. There was a monk called Mendel, who had done something clever with peas and roses, a long time ago. That much I could follow. But when he got on to his

110

own experiments, he forgot he was talking to me. I got lost. His words became longer and longer, and horribly complicated.

I gave up trying to understand, and just watched him. His face looked quite different, no longer old and tired, but alive with interest in what he was telling me. The funny thing was that he reminded me of Monnie then, the way it would stand and whistle at me excitedly, with none of it making any sense.

My father stopped, and smiled ruefully. 'I'm sorry, Frances. I'm afraid I got carried away. Did you understand any of that?'

'I understood the bit about the peas,' I said, 'and you mentioned rice . . . Does that mean you're working on *plants*?'

He smiled. 'Yes. We're trying to improve the yield of certain crops, to make them resistant to disease and extremes of heat and –'

'Plants,' I repeated, with such an enormous sense of relief that I felt dazed.

It must have shown on my face, because he asked curiously, 'What did you think I was doing, Frances?'

'I didn't know.'

That had been the trouble. Every ugly rumour had filled my head with shadowy terrors, until I'd begun to look at my father's ordinary face, and wonder what sort of monster he could be, to do such fearful work. Watching him crack open his breakfast egg, I had half expected the world to explode. And all the time he had been working innocently on rice and wheat and peas.

'Then you don't work with animals at all?' I asked.

'No. Is that what was worrying you, Frances? Animal experiments?'

'Yes,' I said. 'That too, among other things.'

'I see,' he said slowly, 'I know it's a difficult – Frances! Was that why you were afraid to ask me if you could have a pet rabbit? My poor girl, what were you thinking of? Surely you can't have believed that anyone would use his child's pet? For such a purpose? No wonder you ran away if that's what you thought of me!'

'I didn't! I didn't really,' I said quickly, for he looked so horrified. 'It was only . . . I got muddled. People at school say such horrible things about the lab. It's stupid. They call me Frankenstein, and ask me where my monster is. There isn't any monster. There never was. It was only a game we were playing.'

We talked for a long time after that. I think I understand him better now. He can't help seeming stiff and cold. He's shy. Not only with children, with everybody. He said my mother used to tease him about it, saying he only felt safe talking to people in a lecture hall, with a table between him and his audience. I wish I'd known her. He has a photograph of her on his desk. She's laughing, and she looks a little like me when I'm happy. Perhaps one day I will be able to tease him too, and make him laugh.

But not yet.

I told him many things I'd never dreamed I would be able to tell him. How I'd hated it when they whispered about the laboratories at school, how I did not really like being called Frankenstein, though I'd always laughed and pretended not to mind. How the very sight of the laboratories, squatting on the hill above the town, had frightened me, so that I used to turn my head away and not look at them.

But I did not tell him about Monnie.

20

Everything reminded me of Monnie.

My friends tried to comfort me. They came round that first afternoon, with smiling faces and boxes of chocolates.

'Of course Monnie'll be all right, Frankie,' Hazel said. 'Remember how it always loved water. I expect it's having the time of its life in the sea.'

'Of course it'll be able to feed itself,' John said. 'It's a clever little beggar. Look how it got you to that rock. That must've taken some doing. I bet it left you those flowers to say thank you for letting it go.'

'You couldn't have kept her, Frankie,' Alf agreed. 'You did right. She was a water animal, stands to reason with her gills and webbed feet. Don't you worry about her. Tell you what – when I come back from my holiday, I'll let you have two of my rabbits. How about that?'

I did not want rabbits in the hutch where Monnie had lived, but I could not tell him so. He was trying to be kind. They all were.

'Do you think I should tell Dad?' I asked them.

'No,' they all said. 'You can't now. Not after all the lies we've told.'

Now I knew what their story had been. It was hardly flattering to me, making me out to be the sort of silly girl who'd run away in a blind panic, but they were very proud of it. After all, as John pointed out, they had to make it up on the spur of the moment.

'You ought to be grateful, Frankie,' he said.

He had told my father that we'd been playing a monster game and it had got out of hand. He said he and Hazel had put a huge toad in a paper bag, and Julia and I had run off screaming when the bag started hopping across the grass towards us.

John had apologised to my father, saying he had not meant to frighten us so badly – 'I'm sorry, sir,' he'd said. 'It was stupid of me. I should've remembered Frankie's got a thing about monsters and secret weapons. She gets ragged a lot at school. All the kids who've got fathers working at the laboratories do . . .'

I was not surprised that my father had believed John and not Julia. For one thing, Julia had burst into tears and that must have embarrassed him. Also, John has the sort of manners grown-ups like, and an honest-looking face.

'It often comes in useful,' he said.

I smiled, and glanced at Hazel.

'All right, Frankie,' she said. 'It was me. I told them where to look for you. I had to. I couldn't find David anywhere and it was getting late and you didn't come back . . . You could've been murdered! Your dad was worried sick, and so was I. I had to tell him you'd gone off to Didon – Of course I knew! It was painted all over that truck, I'm not blind! I said I didn't know why you'd gone, you seemed terribly upset about something . . . I'm not going to say I'm sorry I told because I'm not, so there! You should've seen your dad's face. He was frantic.'

I told her I didn't blame her. I'd have done the same.

'They wouldn't let me go with them,' she said resentfully. 'It was awful. I didn't know what had happened to you, and I kept wondering if I should've told them about Monnie –'

'I'm sorry, Hazel.'

'I should never have let you go off by yourself. I might've known you'd make a mess of it – Frankie! Frankie, don't look like that! I didn't mean – You know I didn't. Monnie'll be all right. I know it will.'

'Of course it will,' John said, and they both looked at me so anxiously that I had to smile and say I thought so too.

'And don't worry about Julia,' John said. 'She's promised to back our story, and she'd better. I told her just what I'd do if she didn't. To be honest, I don't think it was necessary. She said she regretted it as soon as she'd done it. She really is very sorry, Frankie.' He looked at me from below his long fringe and added, 'She wants to come and see you.'

I did not want to see Julia again. Not ever. It is easier to forgive your enemies than those who pretend to be friends.

'She's waiting in the garden,' John said, watching me. 'Behind the hedge. Crying, I expect. Can I tell her she can come up?'

'If she wants to,' I said grudgingly. What else could I say. I liked John, and she was his sister.

So we forgave Julia. And she did apologise, though in her own way.

'I'm sorry, Frankie, but I only did what I thought was right. After all, you did promise you'd tell Ben. I'd never have agreed to help you otherwise. I mean, your monster could've been dangerous. I only hope it doesn't poison the sea –'

I think John must have kicked her under the table then, for she shut up rather abruptly, and did not say anything else against Monnie. At least, not to me.

Often, in the weeks that followed, I wished I had told my father everything. I could not believe we would

115

get away with it. Too many people had seen me with Monnie; the small girls playing hopscotch, the drunk, the boys in the field above Mendicote woods especially-

I stole the local paper out of Mrs Drake's shopping basket before she had time to read it, but I found nothing in there about a monster and a mad girl, with blood on her face and leaves in her hair. Yet still I felt uneasy. Surely some of them must have told. Perhaps they had and nobody believed them. Perhaps I had frightened them with my threats. I didn't know, and it worried me.

It would spoil everything if my father found out now. He was trying so hard to get to know me. He began taking us out, to the sea or to fly kites in the park. He took us to the theatre in London and to see a new film at the local cinema. At breakfast, he'd leave his paper unopened and try to talk to us about things he thought would interest us. He wasn't very good at it yet. I never understood his jokes, though I laughed politely when I thought he'd made one. He never understood mine either. Not that I made many jokes then.

That was the most difficult thing. I had to pretend to be happy, now that he thought he had explained all my worries away. Sometimes, when I had been silent, thinking about Monnie, I'd look up and find him watching me anxiously, and I'd have to smile. I had to remember not to look round every time a bird whistled behind the high hedge, or cry when I saw a small child playing with a blue ball.

I could not forget Monnie.

And there were bad moments, when I thought everything was going to come out. Once, when I was with my father in the park, we met Professor Blake and his children. I did not like him now. His blue eyes no longer seemed kind and friendly.

116

I kept remembering that Monnie had come from his laboratory, and he'd been going to throw it away. Also I remembered now that David had told me Dad did not approve of some of his experiments. I was frightened of him.

He greeted my father, and then turned to me and said, 'What's all this I hear about your playing monster games, Frances? I should have thought you were too old to be frightened by a joke.' He was smiling, but I thought his eyes looked uncomfortably sharp.

I did not know what to say.

'That's all over now,' my father said quickly, putting his arm round me. I got the impression that he disliked Professor Blake.

'Good, good. I'm glad to hear it,' Professor Blake said, still looking at me. 'It's extraordinary how many new monster stories are going round now. I don't know if you've heard them?'

'No.' I said.

'I only wish my experiments were as successful as people seem to believe,' he went on, still watching me. 'It's a discouraging thought that some great discoveries were made by accident. I shouldn't like to think I'd missed something important.'

I tried to make my face look blank and stupid, and probably succeeded, for he turned away and started talking to my father. I was sure he must have heard something about the boys in Didon, but perhaps it was only my guilty conscience, because he never said any more about it.

I was quiet after he left us. My father smiled at me and said, 'He was only teasing you, Frankie. I'm afraid you're bound to get some of that. Don't worry about it. It's all over now, isn't it?'

'Yes,' I said, and thought about Monnie. If only I could have been sure Monnie was safe and well, I could have been happy.

People were very kind to me, though they must have thought I was a bit crazy or something. Ben and Mike came back from France, and I suppose Dad must have told them what had happened because when they saw me, Ben hugged me and said, 'Well, you are a little idiot, aren't you? If I'd known what silly things you were getting up to, I wouldn't have brought you such a splendid present.'

'Nor me,' Mike said. 'Perhaps we shouldn't give them to her.'

They did, of course. And Alf, when he came back from the Isle of Wight, gave me two rabbits.

They live in the hutch where Monnie used to live. They are soft and pretty, and do not need to have their hands held before they go to sleep. They do not jump up and down and whistle when they see me, they don't bring me small gifts; a feather, a bright pebble or a bunch of wild flowers.

I often went through the woods again to Didon Creek. I'd go with John and Hazel. Not Julia. She had a new friend now, which made life easier.

The three of us would take the bus to Didon, and walk through the fields where I had gone with Monnie. Then we'd climb the gate marked PRIVATE, and make our way down through the trees until we came to the creek. We used to stand on the rocks and call Monnie's name over the quiet water, and listen to the echo reply. Then we'd sit in the sun and talk, and remember.

Once I went by myself. It was a fine April day. I sat on the flat rock overlooking the creek. I did not expect to find Monnie any more, but I liked to sit there and dream. I was growing up. In my teens already, with life opening up before me. I was doing well at school now, and so was Hazel. We were planning to push Julia down into third place . . .

I had come to the creek alone today, because it was time to say a last goodbye.

I can't cry for ever. No one can, I thought, I'll never forget you, Monnie, but it seems like a dream now. If it wasn't for Hazel and John and Alf, I'd think I had imagined you. Perhaps we all imagined you. It was so hot, wasn't it? That summer . . .

Water splashed suddenly against the rocks. I turned round.

A gleaming figure came out of the sea a few yards away. It stood up to its full height, towering above me, and stretched its glittering, metallic arms towards the sky. A ribbed fin, yellow as a cockatoo's crest, grew over its domed head and down between its massive shoulders. Green tendrils fluttered like seaweed from its silvery-wet cheeks.

I stared at it in terror.

It turned its head and looked at me. Its round eyes shone as red as fire. It started jumping up and down and whistling excitedly.

'Monnie?' I whispered, 'Monnie?'

It leaped easily over the rocks between us, and knelt down beside me. It showed me its webbed hands, five fingers on each one, and pointed proudly to its head like someone showing off a new hair style. Its funny slit mouth twisted into a figure eight.

'It's beautiful! You're beautiful,' I said, laughing and clapping my hands. 'Oh Monnie, you're so beautiful. Where have you been? Are you happy? Have you found any friends?'

It pointed to the sea, still whistling, trying to make me understand. It gestured vividly with its hands and I saw dolphins leaping. It spread its huge arms wide and I imagined whales.

We must have been an extraordinary sight, a thin girl and a great shining sea creature, chattering and whistling together, and neither really able to tell what the other was saying. But one thing we both understood without words. We loved one another.

Monnie did not stay long. It was more nervous than it used to be in the garden, and looked round quickly at any unexpected sound. Though it went up to the woods, it did not venture in, but reached up and plucked a twig from an overhanging branch. It looked at it in silence, touching the budding leaves gently with its fingers. I suppose there were no such leaves where it came from, only seaweed and coral. I wondered when it had come back to the creek, and whether it had been waiting for long, hoping to see us.

'Do you ever miss us, Monnie?' I asked, but of course it did not know what I was saying. The pattern of its whistling had changed, as if it had learned to imitate a new language. I thought of dolphins and wondered if they whistled too. I hoped so. I hoped Monnie had found someone to talk to.

It sat beside me for a time, but I noticed it kept glancing towards the sea. Its skin was drying out in the sunlight, and I knew it must go soon.

I did not try to stop it. There was no safe place for Monnie anywhere on land. It was too large and alien and gentle to live among us. It stood up, a huge royal figure with its shining face. Perhaps it would make its own kingdom under the sea, a kinder, friendlier place than we have made on earth.

It pointed to its chest and then towards the sea. I smiled and nodded, held its hands in mine for a moment, then let them go.

'Goodbye, Monnie. Good luck.'

It smiled, whistled high and sweet, and dived into the water. I watched it streak away, leaving a narrow wake like a pale arrow. Then it was gone.

I smiled, and wondered what tales Monnie would carry back to the dolphins. Would it speak, in its weird, whistling language, about a rabbit hutch in a summer garden, about the old man and three children who'd cared for it? And would it tell them about a girl called Frankie, who loved it, and set it free?